THE
RECIPE PROJECT

A Delectable Extravaganza of Food and Music

BY ONE RING ZERO

Published by Black Balloon Publishing
www.blackballoonpublishing.com

Copyright © 2011 by One Ring Zero and contributors
All rights reserved

ISBN-13: 978-1-936787-00-5
ISBN-10: 1-936787-00-8

Black Balloon Publishing titles are distributed to the trade by:
Consortium Book Sales and Distribution
Phone: 800-283-3572 / SAN 631-760X

Library of Congress Control Number: 2011905663

Printed in Hong Kong

9 8 7 6 5 4 3 2 1

First Edition

THE
RECIPE PROJECT
A Delectable Extravaganza of Food and Music
BY ONE RING ZERO

Songs
One Ring Zero

Recipes and More
Mario Batali, John Besh, David Chang, Tom Colicchio, Chris Cosentino, Tanya Donelly, Mark Kurlansky, Isa Chandra Moskowitz, Andrea Reusing, Aarón Sanchez, Michael Symon, Michael Harlan Turkell

Musings
Matthew Amster-Burton, Melissa Clark, Jonathan Dixon, JJ Goode, Christine Muhlke, Emily Kaiser Thelin, Michelle Wildgen, Kara Zuaro

Introduction
John T. Edge

Edited by Michael Hearst and Leigh Newman
Additional Editing by Elizabeth Koch

Black Balloon Publishing
Brooklyn

Contents

P. 6   **Preface**   Leigh Newman

P. 8   **Introduction**   John T. Edge

RECIPES

P. 10   **Spaghetti with Sweet 100 Tomatoes**   courtesy Mario Batali

P. 20   **Peanut Butter Brunettes**   courtesy Isa Chandra Moskowitz

P. 28   **The Ugly Muffin**   Tanya Donelly

P. 30   **Brains and Eggs**   courtesy Chris Cosentino

P. 38   **Raw Peach**   courtesy Mark Kurlansky

P. 52   **Shrimp Remoulade**   courtesy John Besh

P. 60   **Tunisian Tinged Drumsticks**   Michael Harlan Turkell

P. 62   **Maine Jonah Crab Claws with Yuzu Mayonnaise**   courtesy David Chang

P. 72   **Pickled Pumpkin**   courtesy Andrea Reusing

P. 86   **Octopus Salad with Black-Eyed Peas**   courtesy Michael Symon

P. 98   **Creamless Creamed Corn**   courtesy Tom Colicchio

P. 104 **Duck Breast with Dulce de Leche Ancho Chile Glaze**   courtesy Aarón Sanchez

MUSINGS

P. 14 **Love and Caribou** — Christine Muhlke

P. 24 **The Power of Popcake** — Kara Zuaro

P. 44 **Virgin in the Kitchen** — Emily Kaiser Thelin

P. 56 **The Piroshky Effect** — Matthew Amster-Burton

P. 71 **Songs to Lose Customers By** — David Chang

P. 80 **The Order of Desire** — Michelle Wildgen

P. 94 **A Culinary Heretic** — Jonathan Dixon

P. 102 **The Beatles' White Album: I'm Just Here for the Food** — Melissa Clark

P. 108 **A Wine Lover's Guide to Mexican Music** — JJ Goode

INTERVIEWS

P. 34 Chris Cosentino: **Jane's Addiction, Pig Tripe, and Functional Insanity**

P. 42 Mark Kurlansky: **Bach, Fake Rock, and Color-Clashing Vegetables**

P. 66 David Chang: **Fried Chicken, David Bowie, and Girlfriends Who Like *Desperate Housewives***

P. 76 Andrea Reusing: **Bruce Springsteen, Egg Haters, and Giant Clams**

P. 90 Michael Symon: **Raspberries, Moussaka, and Metallica**

P. 110 **Acknowledgments, Liner Notes**

P. 112 **Contents by Page Number**

P. 116 **CD Tracklist**

The Recipe Project began as a musical lark. Michael Hearst and Joshua Camp, co-founders of the band One Ring Zero, decided to turn Chris Cosentino's recipe for Brains and Eggs into a song—word for word, phrase for phrase, including "Remove the brains from the water with a perforated spoon and place on a plate." If that wasn't tricky, or bizarre, enough, they asked Cosentino to recommend a music style. What kind of song would best showcase "light and fluffy" organs served on warm slices of rustic country bread?

"Beastie Boys," replied Cosentino, with a mischievous grin.

So the group set to work, mixing over-saturated drum beats and looped rhythm sequences. "The most daunting task was singing it," says Hearst. "I don't rap. And with such a long list of ingredients, it became a matter of breaking the recipe apart and finding a way to phrase it."

The result was a fast, raucous ode to white-boy hip-hop jams and edible offal that, not surprisingly, caused a fair degree of uncontrollable laughter in the studio. The fact that the

song also highlighted some of Cosentino's more serious culinary concerns—like the importance of cooking with all of an animal's parts, and not just the pretty, more palatable meats—came up only after the recording.

But it was enough to inspire Cosentino to call up a few of his chef friends, like Aarón Sanchez and Michael Symon. They wanted recipe-songs, too. Sanchez preferred a musical homage to banda, the bright, traditional Mexican brass band music. And Symon was all about heavy metal, leading Hearst and Camp to bust out their demonic screaming skills.

It takes a fair degree of talent to thrash out a headbanger version of an octopus salad recipe one week, then whip up a sly, sweet indie-rock gem for "Peanut Butter Brunettes" the next, even convincing Belly's frontwoman Tanya Donelly to lend her vocals to the tune. But the unusual and impossible are trademarks of this hopelessly gifted duo.

The two met in 1995 while working at the Hohner instrument warehouse in Richmond,

Leigh Newman
PREFACE

Virginia, where Hearst tuned harmonicas and Camp repaired accordions. Shortly thereafter, they formed One Ring Zero, a band with a "gypsy-klezmer circus-flea-cartoon" sound, as *The Forward* once described it. Their specialty? Musical curiosities. A single recording session might involve a solo on a theremin (an obscure, early electronic instrument that requires hand-waving around an antenna, but no touching), a stylophone (a toy-like instrument played with a musical "pen"), and a power drill.

And then came the nine albums. For *As Smart as We Are*, Hearst and Camp convinced some of the most celebrated novelists and storywriters in America to write lyrics, which they set to music as songs. *Planets* featured a lineup of songs dedicated to every planet in the solar system. *Alice* played ghostly homage to each chapter of *Alice in Wonderland*. *Songs for Ice Cream Trucks,* created by Hearst as a solo artist, brought to life a thousand hot sticky childhood summers, only with stranger, more bewitching music tinkling through the streets.

And yet, for all its winsome weirdness, *The Recipe Project* hit on some pretty timely debates about food and music: Are America's rock-star chefs actually America's new rock stars? How is all this celebrity affecting the actual food and people that are being celebrated? And why take it all so seriously . . . unless cooking, like hip-hop or TV, is now considered a new national art form? Not to mention: Who put together that insane playlist for David Chang's East Village noodle bar—and who decided to turn it up so loud? (For the answer, see p.71)

(For the answer, see p.71)

Enter Black Balloon Publishing. In starting a new company, co-founder Elizabeth Koch and I were looking for the brilliant and odd, the edgy, dark and delightful—and, most importantly, the ridiculously impossible to explain or sell. *The Recipe Project* had it all, including a dear friend (Hearst) behind the madness.

Our idea: Why not release *The Recipe Project* as a book/CD combo? Why not interview the chefs about their musical proclivities, or lack thereof? (Hint: Michael Symon hates techno.) Why not invite famous food writers to chime in? (Hint: Check out the playlist that bonded *Bon Appetit*'s Christine Muhlke and her husband over caribou marrow.) Why not print the recipe-lyrics so readers can cook the songs at home—or sing them in the car, on the way to work, inspiring their mortified children to slink ever lower in the backseat?

Thus, *The Recipe Project* was born, an extravaganza of food, music, and friendship that brings together chefs, writers, musicians, readers, and listeners—and anybody else in the great big world who believes that sizzling bacon at dawn tastes better with Billie Holiday on the iPod (specifically *Lady in Autumn*). Or that that best way to enjoy a hot, heavenly plate of brains and eggs is with a side of One Ring Zero.

"Chefs are the new rock stars." Reviewers of this slightly whacked food/music/writing project will surely make that observation. One of the messages embedded within the overheated rhetoric is this: Apropos of their new roles within the greater creative world, chefs have earned elevated status.

Food is the currency of the *au courant*. REM's Michael Stipe now pals around with Mario Batali. Notorious MSG, a Chinese rap group based in New York City's Chinatown, wins fist-pumping converts nightly through songs like "Dim Sum Girl" and "Straight out of Canton." Inevitably, *Food is the New Rock,* a blog and Twitter feed, has emerged to catalog the trend and tell us where Flavor Flav will open the next location in his eponymous fast food fried chicken chain.

Recent American history is full of food/music mashups. In the 1970s, James Brown pimped his Golden Platter restaurants. And Conway Twitty tried to sell us on pineapple-topped Twitty Burgers. In the 1980s, the Coolies, an Atlanta band, cut one of my favorite albums of all time, *Doug.* It's a rock opera about a skinhead named Doug—"Schlitz malt liquor is my favorite food/ And pissed off is my favorite mood" —who beats up a restaurant lifer. Pussy Cook, the narrator tells us, worked at the Fish Delight, "Fry cook by day/ Drag queen by night." During the tussle, *Doug* steals Pussy Cook's treasured manuscript and publishes the cookbook to great acclaim before burning up his fortune in the bowl of a crack pipe.

John T. Edge
INTRODUCTION

Doug, which channels both the Who and the Beastie Boys, still plays well. But this time around, the fusion of food and music, as interpreted by One Ring Zero, has gone more literal and instructive.

The band, based in Brooklyn, came to my attention a couple years back when they recorded *As Smart as We Are,* an album featuring lyrics from novelists like Dave Eggers, Jonathan Lethem, Margaret Atwood, and Rick Moody. The songs were playful. ("Kiss Me, You Brat" was Moody's song.) And they were smart.

Critics swooned. Soon One Ring Zero's Michael Hearst—who honed his approach in college by writing a choral piece built around a recitation of grocery store names—began casting about for the band's next opus. He and bandmate Joshua Camp tapped the zeitgeist. And the zeitgeist told them that food was worthy of accordions and guitars and backup singers.

For the last couple of years, One Ring Zero has been working with chefs, setting recipes to music. "It's the ultimate challenge," Hearst told me, soon after they began the project. "To take a list of commands and figure out a way to make it musical."

" In the hands of One Ring Zero, these recipes play like found poetry. "

In the hands of One Ring Zero, these recipes play like found poetry. In many cases, the acts prescribed seem pointedly mundane. Listen as Chris Cosentino poaches and then dices the brains of two calves. Join David Chang as he stirs yuzu into a bowl of Japanese mayonnaise. Visualize Mark Kurlansky, the odd writer in the bunch, as he parts his hair and bites into a ripe and fluent peach.

My son Jess, age ten as of this writing, is partial to track eight. Therein the boys from Brooklyn squall and caterwaul over a Black Sabbath-worthy wall of distortion, while dictating Michael Symon's "Octopus Salad with Black-Eyed Peas." Do we hear Slayer influences? Megadeth? Jess isn't

sure. Neither am I. But the song makes us smile. And as soon as I can get my hands on a whole octopus, I plan to try the dish.

Of course, there's precedent for the One Ring Zero approach, too. Back in the 1970s, Riviana Foods, a Texas-based rice grower and distributor, released an album, *Nashville Chowdown: Country & Western Supper Music and Singing Rice-ipes.* Flatt & Scruggs, Jimmy Dean, and Tammy Wynette were in the mix, crooning standards. Accompanying the LP was a flexi-disk of melodic "rice-ipes"

and a sheet of recipes for, among other delights, Texarkana Rice and Blue Ridge Flap-Jacks.

I don't own it. But my friend James Cury does. He tells me that, on the song "Houston Hash," the lead vocalist sings, in the instructive style of One Ring Zero, "A little woman waits for me in Houston/ Cooks a rice-ipe I really like/ She uses canned tomatoes, ground beef and onions too/ And she mixes it all up with a cup of rice."

John T. Edge *lives in Oxford, Mississippi, where until recently, fiction writer Barry Hannah lived too. "Everything's a failure, when you compare it to music," Hannah once said.*

Mario Batali

We all think we know Mario Batali. He's the brains (and chops) behind an Italian empire of award-winning eateries, including New York landmarks Babbo, Lupa, Otto, and Del Posto, and Vegas mainstays Carnevino and Zefferino. He's the iconic star of Food Network classics like *Molto Mario* and *Iron Chef America.* He's the dude in the rubber shoes scooting around Greenwich Village on his moped. But did you know Batali was once a thespian? In addition to studying Spanish Theatre at Rutgers, he recently debuted in Wes Anderson's *Fantastic Mr. Fox*. Other hobbies include writing spectacular cookbooks, designing cookware, raising funds for children's hunger relief, and revolutionizing (time and time again) the art of Italian cooking in America. Most impressive (to us) — he read every single book by William Faulkner and his restaurant playlists include Tom Waits and Patti Smith.

MARIO★BATALI

Track 01
3:10 Mins

45 RPM

℗ & © 2011 One Ring Zero, Black Balloon. All rights reserved.

M. Batali,
M. Hearst
& J. Camp

SPAGHETTI
★ WITH ★
SWEET 100
TOMATOES

Produced by
One Ring
Zero

Kosher salt
1/4 cup extra-virgin olive oil
4 garlic cloves, thinly sliced
1 pint sweet 100 tomatoes,
or other tiny tomatoes

1/2 bunch garlic chives,
cut into 1-inch lengths
12 fresh lemon basil leaves,
finely shredded
Freshly ground black pepper, to taste
1 pound spaghetti

---

1. Bring 6 quarts of water to a boil and add 2 tablespoons of salt.

2. In a 12- to 14-inch sauté pan, heat the olive oil over high heat until almost smoking. Lower the heat to medium-high and add the garlic cloves. Cook for 2 minutes, or until softened and slightly browned. Add the tomatoes, chives, and basil, and cook over high heat until the tomatoes are just beginning to burst. Season with salt and pepper.

3. Meanwhile, cook the spaghetti in the boiling water according to package directions until it is tender, yet al dente. Drain the pasta and add it to the pan with the tomatoes. Toss over high heat for 1 minute, then divide evenly among four warmed pasta bowls and serve immediately.

SERVES 4

About six months after I began dating the man who would become my husband, I discovered iTunes. Work aside, it was the only thing that could keep me away from him for hours at a time. My first dinner mix—not to be confused with my harder, faster sets—debuted at our first dinner party. Over the next seven years, our parties featured some crucial staples: Aviation cocktails (gin,

Christine Muhlke

LOVE & CARIBOU

maraschino, lemon juice) to get people drunk enough that they don't realize it's 9:15 and they haven't eaten; the rice pudding from L'Ami Jean in Paris, which I wrote about in order to get the recipe; and a playlist of goofy and forgotten songs.

Here are some past mixes, along with meals served and remembered.

> **" Oliver and I have a lot in common entertaining-wise: We both go to the B.H.P. (Bad Hostess Place). "**

Dinner 1: February 2004

Even though he has cooked professionally and is, at the time, cooking privately, I learn the night of our first dinner party that Oliver and I have a lot in common entertaining-wise: We both go to the B.H.P. (Bad Hostess Place). Seeing him melt down over the gougères 15 minutes before our friends arrive cures me of the tendency. My melting down on his meltdown cures him of his.

He nails a huge pot of bouillabaisse, complete with rich fish stock and garlicky rouille. I am still in a dedicated Claudia Fleming phase and can't tear myself away from her individual tartes tatin, no matter that I get in Oliver's way, heat up the kitchen, and never fail to burn myself. As for the music, I strategically put "Maps" at the end because it's a good make-out song—the better to interrupt your dishwashing—and it hadn't yet become a cliché.

The takeaway: the dishes can always wait until the morning.

	The Playlist	
1	*Tico Tico*	**Andrews Sisters**
2	*My Heart Belongs to Daddy*	**Anita O'Day**
3	*Give Him the Ooh-La-La*	**Blossom Dearie**
4	*Maria Ninguen*	**Brigitte Bardot**
5	*Like a Rolling Stone (live)*	**Bob Dylan**
6	*Me and My Shadow*	**Frank Sinatra & Sammy Davis Jr.**
7	*Mañana*	**Peggy Lee**
8	*Mini, amini, mini*	**Jacques Dutronc**
9	*Hey Cowboy*	**Lee Hazlewood**
10	*Do I Move You?*	**Nina Simone**
11	*Baby (1971)*	**Os Mutantes**
12	*Country Honk*	**The Rolling Stones**
13	*Blinuet*	**Zoot Sims**
14	*Maps*	**Yeah Yeah Yeahs**

Dinner IV: January 2006

My friend Alex is moving to Paris for six months, so Oliver and I host her going away party. After two years of hosting together, we're developing patterns and checklists, learning to skip a course or two. I've become the apartment cleaner, front of house and dessert maker. Oliver is the talent. He mans the panini press. (He'd been cooking backstage at fashion shows and realized that models kill for croque monsieurs with real béchamel. Once, when she came back for seconds, the Italian model Mariacarla Boscono told him about how much she loved the food on a recent shoot in Rome: "I hate and I hate! Oh, I hate so much!") I make a double recipe of port-glazed walnuts with Stilton. I'm not sure how I got the three feet of pizzas from Sullivan Street Bakery—zucchini, mushroom, bianca—home on my bike. Nor am I sure how we managed to go through 10 bottles of Champagne, a bottle of gin, two bottles of vodka and some regifted cachaça. One woman, looking out my window, realizes that an ex of hers lives across the way. There he was, shirtless, on command. By the time "Moi Je Joue" comes on, one of my colleagues is flirting with an ex of mine. We all stumble out into the cold and get another round at Marie's Crisis.

I put E.L.O. on this mix for Alex, because she was my rock-block, car-singing dream date. I put "Religious Man," from the brilliant movie *Nacho Libre*, on here for her, too. We saw it as a joke the night it opened and laughed so hard that spiked Sprite came out of our noses. Fast forward: Alex has lived in Paris for almost five years. Oliver now makes the Sullivan Street pizzas himself thanks to that awesome Jim Lahey book. My colleague and my ex are still dating. I understand the world about 13% less.

The Playlist

1	*Let's Make Love*	Frankie Vaughan, Marilyn Monroe & Yves Montand
2	*Dance Rock 'n Roll*	Benjamin Biolay & Chiara Mastroianni
3	*Tive Razao (I Was Right)*	Seu Jorge
4	*Interior of a Dutch House*	Beirut
5	*It's a Living Thing*	Electric Light Orchestra
6	*Dearie's Blues*	Blossom Dearie
7	*Hombre Religioso (Religious Man)*	Mr. Loco
8	*Tu Vuo' Fa L'Americano*	Fiorello
9	*Mrs. Robinson*	Frank Sinatra
10	*Ring of Fire*	Bob Dylan and Johnny Cash
11	*Wear Your Love Like Heaven*	Donovan
12	*Samtbraune Augen*	Hildegard Knef
13	*Desafinado (Slightly Out of Tune)*	Julie London
14	*Tell Me Now So I Know*	Holly Golightly
15	*Moi Je Joue*	Brigitte Bardot
16	*Let's Make Love (Reprise)*	Yves Montand

Dinner VII: May 2008

Oliver now spends a lot of time hunting with Canadians, and he is a changed man. A beard? A rifle? I love listening to the stories of what he and his hunting pals, major cooks in Montreal, cook at camp—beaver burgers (I am assuming this is a dish and not a metaphor), caribou, moose marrow. Inspired by all the game in our freezer, I inexplicably invite Judith Jones to dinner. The 80-something editor—she who discovered Julia Child in the '60s, who brought us Marcella Hazan, Madhur Jaffrey, Edna Lewis—worked on the L.L. Bean game cookbook in the '80s, a copy of which I bought after I wrote a story in which I cooked her cassoulet. (A very fun disaster.) No pressure. Oliver orders a guinea hen and plans to braise it for five hours, as per the *Au Pied du Cochon* cookbook. There will be a puree of something, and I'll do that rice pudding.

There is a freak heat wave.

The day of the party, it is 95 degrees and the oven has been on since noon. We do not reverse course and make ceviche and gazpacho. By the time Judith arrives, the oven has been on for basically ever. Oliver changes his shirt twice during the meal, which is good not great. (Guinea fowl is tough!) Judith is a trooper, a true, uncomplaining WASP. I end up sending her a thank you note.

Oliver and I are getting married in five months, but I've already started putting together the slow-dancers that make my throat tighten: "All the Things You Are," "It Was You" and, as a nose-thumbing fuck you to the loneliness of high school, "Thieves Like Us."

	The Playlist	
1	*Thieves Like Us*	**New Order**
2	*Brother Jack (Frère Jacques) [Take 3]*	**Manfred Mann**
3	*All the Things You Are*	**Ella Fitzgerald**
4	*Embrasse-Moi*	**Jeanne Moreau**
5	*Climb Up on My Music*	**Rodriguez**
6	*All Along the Watchtower*	**Bob Dylan**
7	*Laisse-Moi*	**Chantal Goya**
8	*Bandian*	**Balla et ses**
9	*Samba Saravah Pierre Barouh*	**from "Un homme et une femme"**
10	*Human Racing*	**St. Vincent**
11	*It Was You (Aretha Arrives Outtake)*	**Aretha Franklin**
12	*Too Drunk to F**k*	**Nouvelle Vague**
13	*Why Can't I Touch It?*	**Buzzcocks**
14	*Canadian Girl*	**The Walkmen**
15	*What's New*	**Ahmad Jamal**

A few weeks after we were married, Oliver killed a caribou. To celebrate, we had two very insane meals. The New Year's dinner for six consisted of five caribou courses. Because the meat was so clean (caribou eat only lichen), we weren't even sleepy by the fifth. For dessert I made a Fané, an elegantly addictive ice-cream dessert that requires at least four more hours in the freezer than I allotted for. Next year.

A month later, Oliver decides he's ready: he's going to cook caribou for Eric Ripert, the chef of Le Bernardin. I'd written a book with Eric a year before and had wanted to have him over to thank him. It took us that long to work up the courage.

The menu for that night's meal is still taped to a cupboard:

CARIBOU TARTARE
1) Dressing • 2) Salad • 3) Toast

⋮

CARIBOU TENDERLOIN CHOP

⋮

CARIBOU TENDERLOIN
1) Wine reduction • 2) Salad

⋮

CARIBOU SHANK
1) Herbs

⋮

CARIBOU ROAST LEG
1) Herbs • 2) Mushrooms • 3) Potatoes + chokes

At midnight the night before the meal, we have to sneak over to a meat processor with the caribou bones in a tote bag to have them sliced vertically, rather than across, for the marrow. It was the way Oliver had seen it done at Au Pied du Cochon in Montreal with a moose, and besides, we didn't have those little marrow spoons. (The processor, who does the meat for chic restaurants, now cuts marrow bones this way, which cracks me up every time I see it.)

There is a messy snowstorm. Eric and his wife arrive bundled and booted. We start with an Aviation, and things take off from there. The food is perfection, the wine is memorable. And yes, I made that rice pudding again and everyone asks for the recipe. Honest. Because the meal is so long, the conversation is one of those that just gets deeper and funnier, building upon itself. At one point, Eric turns to me and says, "Il peut cuisinier, Oliver. Ce n'est pas du bullshit." By the end of the night, it feels like everyone knows and likes each other better. It is, we realize, the perfect mix.

Christine Muhlke is executive editor of Bon Appetit. *For seven years, she was deputy editor at* T Magazine *and the food editor of* The New York Times Magazine.

The Playlist

#	Title	Artist
1	*Roll Over Beethoven*	**Electric Light Orchestra**
2	*Knotty Pine*	**David Byrne & Dirty Projectors**
3	*Could You Be the One?*	**Hüsker Dü**
4	*Daylight*	**Matt & Kim**
5	*My Generation*	**Patti Smith**
6	*My Last Mistake*	**Dan Auerbach**
7	*Histoire à Suivre*	**The Honeymoon Killers** *[the Belgian ones]*
8	*Needles in the Camel's Eye*	**Brian Eno**
9	*Damaged Goods*	**Gang Of Four**
10	*Oh Oh Oh Oh Oh Oh Oh*	**Say Hi**
11	*Freakin Out*	**Death**
12	*Je Danse Le Mia (Platinum Collection)*	**IAM**
13	*This Is Radio Clash*	*The Clash* **I Got a Right (1973)**
14	*Original Siamese single)*	**Iggy Pop & The Stooges**
15	*Cravo é Canela*	**Tortoise and Bonnie "Prince" Billy**
16	*Just Like Heaven*	**Dinosaur Jr.**

Isa Chandra Moskowitz,

author of *Vegan with a Vengeance* and four other best-selling
vegan cookbooks, takes a winsome approach to hard-core
veganism—cupcakes, tweets, and pure personality. She issued
a call to bake-sale action on her blog and raised $75,000
for Haiti. Her New York-based cooking show, *Post Punk
Kitchen* (now off-air) blended punk-rock sentiments with easy
vegan recipes (Pumpkin-Crusted Tofu, anyone?) and tapped
into an anarcho-foodie subculture that had been seriously
underestimated. She likes bird-watching, board games, and
cooking up trouble on the Lower East Side. In case you're
wondering, it wasn't politics or anti-capitalist persuasions
that turned her vegan. It was love—for her cat, Fizzle.

ISA CHANDRA MOSKOWITZ

45 RPM

Track 02
2:36 Mins

PEANUT BUTTER
BRUNETTES
I. Moskowitz, J. Camp & M. Hearst
Guest Vocals: T. Donelly
Produced by One Ring Zero

3/4 cup peanut butter
1/3 cup canola oil
1 cup brown sugar
1/4 cup almond milk
2 teaspoons vanilla extract

1 cup all-purpose flour
1/2 teaspoon salt
1/2 teaspoon baking powder
1/3 cup peanuts

Preheat oven to 350 degrees.

Mix together peanut butter, oil, sugar, milk, and vanilla. Stir in flour, salt, and baking powder. Transfer to an 8x8 metal baking pan and press it into place. Sprinkle on the peanuts.

Bake for 22 to 25 minutes. Let cool and cut into squares.

SERVES 4

Be careful about asking a man in a touring band about his mother's cooking. Actually, be careful when asking any man about his mother's cooking—the mere question may stir up unprecedented emotion and remind him that he needs a woman in his life to cook and care for him, while he is drunkenly staring into your eyes—but the touring musician is especially vulnerable. He is weakened by nights spent on strangers' floors, and he hasn't had a home-cooked meal in ages. Remind him of his mother, and you may not be able to get rid of him. I spent a few years asking many a musician about food for a cookbook I was writing about what bands ate on the road. Inevitably, Mom came up. Whether I wanted her to or not.

Kara Zuaro
THE POWER OF POPCAKE

Take the case of the scruffy Chicago band Catfish Haven. The band was named after the Illinois trailer park in which frontman George grew up. It was there that his mother Maria started making him Strawberry Popcake for his birthday every year. The hot pink confection involves a stick of butter, four eggs, strawberry soda, a box of cake mix, a packet of instant pudding, a packet of strawberry Jell-O, and Cool Whip on top. And by the way, George is a deep-voiced man with a thick beard, torn jeans, and straight dark hair that hangs halfway down his back. He just happens to have an appetite like a Malibu Barbie with the munchies.

A few years ago my husband, Pete—who was just my boyfriend at the time—took me to see Catfish Haven while I was mourning the death of Otis Redding. His plane went down in 1967, twelve years before I was born, but I was so caught up in soul music history in my mid-twenties that the loss felt current and personal. I took solace in Catfish Haven's soulful sound, and after the show, I learned that George was as big a fan as I was. We chatted about our favorite live recordings, swapped fun facts about Redding's life. As we walked through the cold Brooklyn night toward an after-hours bar, I asked George if he knew that Otis was only 26 when he died. He took off his fogged-up glasses as if to wipe them clean, but rubbed his sleeve across his eyes. George and I were both 26 that winter, and in that misty-eyed moment of shared love for a fallen hero, our friendship was sealed. Before I started to tear up, too, I asked him to tell me more about his mama's Popcake.

Before long, I had his mother Maria's phone number in my pocket. When I called, she told me all about George's childhood and described a little rake for the sandbox that she bought him when he was a toddler and that he used to mimic his father's guitar-playing. "He was so cute, jamming with that little yellow rake—it was his air guitar for the longest time," Maria said. "We bought him a child's guitar when he was about four, but that guitar didn't sound the same as what was in his head when he played that little rake." From that point on, I couldn't see George as another grubby indie rock frontman—I saw a sweet baby boy with a plastic yellow rake. I started rolling into Catfish shows with baked goods. In the course of my recipe collecting, I spoke to a bunch of band mothers. Although I was asking about their cooking, I was also trying to figure out how

As I sit here today, I'm typing over a belly as ripe as a watermelon. I thought I'd be one of those pregnant gals who got really into prenatal yoga and cute maternity clothes. Instead, I find myself sipping non-alcoholic beer in a stretched out Cursive t-shirt, and running around to rock shows and restaurants to finish my writing and reviewing assignments. On a daily basis, I belt out Townes Van Zandt's "Delta Momma Blues" to my unborn child—never mind that the song has more to do with tripping on Robitussin DM than the joys of motherhood—and wonder if his kicking means he's cheering or begging me to shut up already.

" George just happens to have an appetite like a Malibu Barbie with the munchies. "

they raised their kids. What turns a baby boy into a musician? Peggy Herweg, the mother of Larry and Bryan Herweg of Chicago's Pelican, enriched cakes with oatmeal and blasted The Marshall Tucker Band to quell the screaming of her colicky babies. San Francisco singer-songer John Vanderslice's mother, Jean Young, baked fruit crumble and cried when her son told her he wanted to be an artist instead of a businessman—she was so proud of him and couldn't believe that she'd raised someone so brave. The mother of Ed Droste from Brooklyn's Grizzly Bear bakes a pecan pie a la mode whenever he goes home. After our talks, I felt so strangely close to these women—even though I didn't have any kids of my own.

I may never be an expert on nursery rhymes or knitting booties, but a few months before I got pregnant, I got a taste of what being a mom might be like. My husband Pete works in the music industry and it's not uncommon to have a tour-worn band passing through our apartment. I cook, Pete entertains, and for a little while, our family feels bigger, our home feels full. But the last time Catfish Haven appeared was a bit different. We hadn't spoken to them in months, so I was surprised when Pete barged into the bathroom during my late-afternoon shower to tell me, "Um, Catfish Haven is here."

"Where?" I asked, peeking out of the shower curtain. Pete looked alarmed. He shut the bathroom door behind him.

"They're upstairs. Their van broke down in West Virginia a couple of days ago and they've been carrying their gear on a Greyhound for a couple of days. It's a bad scene."

"Okay," I said. "I can make spaghetti."

"I think they need to eat now," Pete said. There was an unfamiliar note of urgency in his voice. "I'm ordering Thai food—you want spicy noodles?"

"Sure," I said. "Are they okay?"

"I don't know. I need back-up."

At times like these, you realize that the one leg you shaved will have to suffice. We'd been planning to go to their show that night—we just hadn't anticipated seeing them beforehand. I mopped myself off, put on some sweats as I climbed the stairs to our living room. I stopped. It was as though a dumpster had been emptied in our home—a New York City summertime dumpster, brimming with boiling rotten fruit, sour milk, rank fish bones. My stomach lurched. George, Ryan, and Miguel were piled on the couch, eyes bloodshot, scowling silently. Pete was playing an acoustic guitar on a chair. When George stood up to hug me, I held my breath and gave him a squeeze.

It was pouring out and the boys were as wet as I was. They weren't sure how many days they'd spent transferring from Greyhound to Greyhound, and when they finally made it to their friend's house in Williamsburg, he told them they couldn't stay there because he was recording another band in his home studio. They'd taken a couple of trains to our place—carrying their instruments on their backs. I poured some water and lit a candle, but its lavender scent was no match for the stench.

"Why don't you guys take showers while we wait for the food?" I suggested. "I've got plenty of towels." But they'd left their spare clothes in the van in West Virginia—all they had was what they had on. "We're not showering on this tour anyway," George said, smiling a little. "It's the first tour when all three of us are single."

"Wouldn't you have a better shot at meeting some ladies if you got cleaned up?" I asked.

"No, we're working on our pheromones," George said. "Some girls like it a little musky."

"Pheromones are not the same thing as B.O." I said. "Guys, if you don't take a shower, you could get a fungus or something."

"Don't worry," George assured me. "I'm still washing my crotch area." All of a sudden he stood up from the table and gracefully motioned toward his "crotch area" with both hands, like a bowler making a slow-motion victory gesture after throwing a strike.

The doorbell rang, signaling the arrival of Thai food, and they dove into it like animals. Instead of dessert, I suggested a nap before their show.

They didn't want to take a nap.

I proceeded to light all the candles and incense I could find and covered our couches with my old pink sheets. I inflated our air mattress and covered it in pink as well. I fluffed pillows and slid them into fresh cases. George reminded me that they weren't going to take a nap.

like to be a mother of sons—overwhelmed with love for cranky, smelly people who just want to be left alone.

I thought back to my chat with George's mom, Maria, and what she would do for her son, sitting upstairs. Then I thought: How will I know how to soothe my own son one day? What will this kid be like? What kind of mother will I be? Will I blast classic rock when he cries? Will I bake his birthday cakes from scratch? Will he miss my cooking when he's far from home?

" I stared at them for a moment, overwhelmed by the desire to buy them new socks and underwear. "

"Oh, it's no trouble at all," I said, passive-aggressively dimming the lights, and turning on a mostly-silent nature show about sunrises. With the sound of ocean waves lapping from the speakers behind me, I said, "I'm going to go downstairs and blow-dry my hair, so just let me know if you change your mind about the shower."

I stared at them for a moment, overwhelmed by the desire to buy them new socks and underwear at the 5 and 10 around the corner. I've never wanted to do a load of laundry more in my life. If only they would listen to me, I could bake them cookies while they showered and slept and everything would be fine. I felt like a crazy person. In my head, I thought, "I'm doing this because I care about you." But I didn't say anything aloud. I wondered if this is what it felt

Sure, Marshall Tucker, Townes Van Zandt, and Hickory Dickory Dock may cut it while he's a baby, but what happens when he grows up, when he comes home reeking of heartbreak, his band falling apart, his eyes teary under a pair of fogged-up glasses? In my pantry there's a lot of dried chickpeas, wholesome wheatberries, and homemade chili powder. Maybe it's time to keep it stocked with strawberry soda, boxed cake mix, instant pudding, and strawberry Jell-O. So Popcake isn't organic. It isn't vitamin-rich. But its magical healing powers have been proven by mothers before me. ⁝⁝

Kara Zuaro *is a freelance writer and the author of* I Like Food, Food Tastes Good: In the Kitchen with Your Favorite Bands.

Tanya Donelly
THE UGLY MUFFIN

The Grammy-nominated singer-songwriter and guitarist Tanya Donelly entranced alternative rock fans with her bands the Throwing Muses, The Breeders, and Belly. Now a solo artist, mother, and postpartum doula, Donelly takes food seriously. Especially kid food. In her own words:

" This is not a pretty muffin, but really good and (mostly) good for you. And also a good way to slip veggies, fruits, fiber, and antioxidants into people (four-year-olds and similar) who are normally resistant to such things. If still met with resistance, frost it and try again. "

2 cups all-purpose flour
1 cup oat bran
3/4 cup brown sugar
1 teaspoon baking soda
1 teaspoon baking powder
1 teaspoon salt
1/4 cup skim milk
1/2 cup spinach/blueberry puree (right)
2 eggs, beaten
1 teaspoon vanilla extract

2 tablespoons vegetable oil
2 apples, peeled and shredded
1 1/2 cups dark chocolate chips

For spinach/blueberry puree:
1 1/2 cups raw baby spinach leaves
3/4 cup fresh blueberries
1 tablespoon water
Puree all in food processor until smooth.

Preheat oven to 350 degrees. Lightly oil or butter a muffin pan, or line with paper liners.

Mix together flour, oat bran, brown sugar, baking soda, baking powder, and salt. In a separate bowl, mix together milk, spinach/blueberry puree, eggs, vanilla, and oil. Then add liquid mixture to dry mixture and mix until just blended. Stir in the apples and chocolate chips. Fill the prepared muffin cups 2/3 full with batter.

Bake at 350 degrees for 15 to 20 minutes, or until a toothpick inserted into the center of a muffin comes out clean.

Let cool. Eat.

Chris Cosentino,

executive chef of San Francisco's Incanto, competitor on *The Next Iron Chef,* and founder of Boccalone artisanal meats, is wild about meat. Not the usual kind that "comes in color-coded Styrofoam at your local supermarket." The other kind. Abdominal organs and extremities. Brains and tongue. Tails and feet. The stuff butchers generally let fall off the carcass, collectively called offal. Little does the general public know, he also makes a mean, green vegan menu. No joke.

CHRIS ★ COSENTINO

45 RPM

Track 03
2:47 Mins

BRAINS
AND EGGS
C. Cosentino, M. Hearst & J. Camp
Produced by One Ring Zero

2 calves brains
1 teaspoon salt
1 tablespoon lemon juice
1 tablespoon white wine

5 eggs
2 tablespoons cream

1 tablespoon butter
1 teaspoon chopped chives
1 teaspoon chopped tarragon
4 slices of rustic country bread
2 teaspoons extra virgin olive oil
Salt to taste
Black pepper to taste

To poach the brains, fill a large pot with water and add the salt, lemon juice, and white wine. Bring the water to a boil and then turn it down to a simmer, so the water is lightly bubbling. Gently place the brains into the water and simmer them for 5 minutes. Remove the brains from the water with a perforated spoon and place on a plate. Put the plate in the refrigerator to cool for about 15 minutes.

In a mixing bowl, combine the eggs, cream, and herbs and beat with a whisk until light. Season with salt and black pepper. Set in the refrigerator until ready to use.

Once the brain is cold and firm, dice it. Heat the butter in a sauté pan over high heat until it starts to brown. Then add the cubed brain pieces and gently stir until golden brown. Turn the heat down to medium. Pour in the egg mixture and fold the brains and eggs together with a rubber spatula until it's all cooked; it will be light and fluffy.

While the eggs are cooking, grill or toast the bread so it will be warm when the eggs are finished. Serve the brains on warm plates with a piece of buttered toast.

SERVES 4

CHRIS COSENTINO
JANE'S ADDICTION, PIG TRIPE, AND FUNCTIONAL INSANITY

TRP: How do you come up with new dishes? Do you feel there is any correlation with song composition?

CC: I wouldn't know. I'm not a musician. I hated music class. They used to make me play the fucking recorder and I wanted to kill myself.

TRP: I had to play the maracas.

CC: We had no choice but to play the same stupid shit. The thing about cooking and music, though—I wouldn't say it's about making flavors and colors and textures. Mark Miller [James Beard-award-winning chef of Coyote Cafe] was instrumental in explaining this to me. When you go out and listen to music, does this interest you: daaahdahh daahhdaaaaahhhhhhh. Does that interest you at all? No, it doesn't. So why would a meal interest you if it sounded the same way, if what was going on with your palate, if the appearance of the food was just daaahdahhdah daaaaaaahhh. You know?

TRP: Good analogy. If every song sounds exactly the same—

CC: People don't pay attention anymore, it becomes monotonous, it becomes boring. In a restaurant you should have a flurry of different things. It's like when you listen to the music that goes dah-DAH! dah-DAH-DAH-DAH! dah. Your attention is kept. The same thing applies when you're cooking. You need to hit all the senses. Music just elicits a reaction from a different set of senses. This is what I truly understand as composition, whether it's food or music.

TRP: Does the same idea apply to the composition of a tasting menu? How do you to keep the progression of dishes varied—like an album, full of slow make-out dishes and fast-dance dishes?

CC: We don't do tasting menus here. I don't believe in dictating what a guest should eat. But when it comes to ebb and flow of food, I really like the concept of going with the biggest item first and the lightest thing last. Most albums are set up like that. You get a big punch in the mouth with the first song on the CD, and then you kind of find your way through things you're not familiar with, and then in the middle there's a big wallop and it kind of tapers down. The goal is keeping people excited and enticed by what you're doing. It doesn't always have to be big and bold and in your face, and I think subtlety goes a long way.

TRP: A lot of times the appetizers are the most exciting plates on the menu. The most experimental.

CC: You know what it is, people don't blink an eye at paying between $10 or $15 for something they've never had before that's totally unique. But when you price it at $23, people are like, oh fuck, there's no way in hell I'm going to pay that for my entrée, I don't know what the fuck that's going to taste like. It's

having a super-refined 20-piece band, and then they'll do something that's totally acapella or completely freeform. That's the comparison, where you have freeform solo Grandma style, and a super-refined 20-piece band, on the same album—showing variance in their ability and their skill. And it's kind of the same with restaurant makers.

TRP: Music is usually thought of as an art. What about cooking?

CC: Just like music, you first need to know how to play the instrument or hold a tune. First you learn the craft, which builds the legs to stand on, then you can mix it with art to create your own style. Everyone needs to start with the basic cooking techniques before they can create.

" I really don't care about safety or perfection. I do whatever I want, when I want. "

a certain mentality. The perception is that I'm buying this as an entrée, it's gotta be the fucking best thing I ever had, and I'm not gonna pay over X dollars for it. Which to me is a little ridiculous.

I really don't care about safety or perfection. I do whatever I want, when I want. I'll have super-ornate, detailed fancy dishes, and then very rustic ones, like Grandma put it together. It's like

TRP: You like to ride fixed-gear bikes. Is there a correlation with no-brakes, full-speed ahead dishes? It seems kind of like a life philosophy.

CC: I like riding a single speed mountain bike because there is no one to blame but yourself. No extra parts to break. You rely on yourself. It's kind of the same for food, I want the product to speak for itself, in all its forms.

TRP: Quick question: olive oil or butter?

CC: (laughs)

TRP: Stones or Beatles?

CC: (laughs)

TRP: Brains or tripe?

CC: I don't pick favorites.

TRP: Name the one thing in the world that you would never, ever eat, because . . . uh . . . it's just too gross.

CC: I don't like stinky tofu, the fermentation flavor is too strong for me. I also don't like balut—it's a fully formed duck egg, fermented then hard-boiled. You eat it feathers and all.

TRP: What about bands?

CC: I don't like country or The Grateful Dead, that's for sure. Add Phish in there, too. But then, you never know what a group might end up doing.

TRP: Or a chef.

CC: Yeah. Perception versus reality. There is always this perception of what the chef or musician is supposed to do, or trying to do, and then there is the reality of what they really do. That's a pretty powerful thing. Whether we're talking a guest in a restaurant, or a consumer buying an album, the perception may be one thing, and the reality another. People may not know that a particular musician was classically trained or can play 10 instruments. Maybe in reality he plays every single instrument on the goddamn album, and only hires a band to do the actual show. For me, unfortunately, the world thinks all I do is serve bags of guts and blood cocktails, when in reality it's just a minimal part of what I do. I'm a firm believer in using everything. I'll have vegans say they had the best vegan meal they ever had in their life—in an all-meat restaurant. So the perception vs the reality is a very interesting dynamic.

And I'm sure for a lot of musicians out there, they get this too. A perfect example is with Jane's Addiction or Perry Farrell. His next band Satellite Party came out of nowhere and sounded not a thing like his earlier stuff. It threw everybody for a loop. A lot of people backlashed against Satellite Party, but he was having fun. I think sometimes screwing with people's expectations, whether in music or in the kitchen, is a lot of fun. Unfortunately the world doesn't want everybody to have a good time, they want what they want.

TRP: They want what they've decided you are.

CC: They're dictating what the chef or musician is before they really know who that person is. Does that make sense?

TRP: Yeah. But there's an advantage to this, isn't there. Like when you're making a vegan meal, and you're supposed to be this offal specialist, it must feel like you've got this guilty secret, this surprise. It's an exciting place to play around in.

CC: There's something to be said for keeping people on their toes. It's a very hard dynamic. Whether they admit to it or not, every musician has somebody that influenced them when they were younger. And every chef has somebody that influenced them, when they were younger—and somebody who has inspired them recently.

TRP: No doubt you're inspiring somebody right now.

CC: I don't know if I inspire anybody (laughs). It's really not my goal.

TRP: What about the other way around? Have you been thinking about someone's work lately?

CC: Not really. I just think that every day you have to look at yourself and to replicate that meal? No, I don't. But did it kick me in the ass and make me think a little bit more? Yes. And I think that's the same thing with musicians, they're always looking for that fire, those little moments of passion. A girlfriend kicked them to the curb, or somebody, you know, hit their fucking car. Or they got strung out on fucking heroin for nine days straight and saw Jesus Christ and Moses at the same table with that is? And it never fucking ends.

Music, that's a different insanity. You can turn off music, you can get off stage and not play. Restaurant work never ends. I'm feeding people. I'm nourishing people. People are impatient for it. If a musician is 45 minutes late, people wait. If I made you wait 45 minutes for a table, you'd freak out and demand a free bottle of wine or slam me on Yelp.

> " *Screwing with people's expectations, whether in music or in the kitchen, is a lot of fun.* "

wonder if you've pushed things to the next level. Sometimes I eat a beautiful Japanese meal that's super simple and just, wow, classic, and it makes me wonder: am I going too far, or not far enough? Things influence you whether you realize it or not. Sometimes just little moments you can't even pinpoint until much later. It's a very hard thing. I think a lot of chefs are brilliant, very talented, they've cooked meals that knocked my socks off. Do I want to emulate that meal? No, I don't. Do I want a pink elephant, and it created this new album for them. They always say that brilliance is the borderline of insanity. Creativity is that same borderline of insanity.

TRP: So how do you stay on this side of the border?

CC: Actually I think you don't. To make something that's really gonna affect people, you have to push it, you have to focus the adrenaline rush. Do you know how hard But this is what I signed up for. If I'd wanted to be an artist, I would have gone to art school and thrown some paint around.

I'm not reinventing the wheel here, I'm just trying to make good food. All I ever really wanted to do was be a chef. A cook. Not even own a restaurant. Not be in charge of an empire of restaurants. If I make myself insane in the process, that's my choice.

Mark Kurlansky

writes novels, journalism, radio plays, philosophical inquiries, and children's books. Oh . . . and he also writes about food, in little smash bestsellers like *Salt, Cod*, and *The Basque History of the World*. Along the way, he's collected an enviable smattering of accolades. Think the James Beard Award for Food Writing, induction to the Basque Hall of Fame, *Bon Appetit* magazine's Food Writer of the Year and The Glenfiddich Award. His secret dream? To date Anna Karenina.

MARK KURLANSKY

Track 04
0:56 Mins

45 RPM

RAW
★★★
PEACH

M. Kurlansky, J. Camp & M. Hearst
Produced by One Ring Zero

Raw Peach

1. You should part your hair behind.
2. Dare to eat it.
3. Hold the peach in front of your mouth.
4. Bite in.
5. And indeed there will be time.

SERVES 1

MARK KURLANSKY
BACH, FAKE ROCK, AND COLOR-CLASHING VEGETABLES

TRP: What inspired your recipe, "Raw Peach?"

MK: Well, clearly T.S. Eliot did.

TRP: You mean the line from "The Love Song of J. Alfred Prufrock?" "Do I dare to eat a peach?" Did you listen to a lot of poetry, growing up? What about music?

MK: As a child, I listened almost exclusively to classical music because that was what my parents listened to. They in particular loved opera, and radio broadcasts from the Met such as "Your Box at the Opera" were important events. My father was a dentist and anyone who got their teeth fixed by Dr. Kurlansky knew they would get opera along with the drill. He also produced children's opera for the industrial area on the edge of Hartford where we lived.

Listening to classical music is the best way to learn music and it is why later, when I was moved by diverse forces such as Miles Davis and Jimi Hendrix, I could appreciate what they were doing.

TRP: What kind of music do you listen to now in the kitchen?

MK: I generally like to listen to Caribbean music when I cook—Cuban, Jamaican, Guadeloupe, Trinidad, Dominican. But I also listen to Motown. I listen to music with a good dance beat because it imposes a rhythm, which is important when you are cooking. One of the leading varieties of bad food is the over-wrought food celebrated on the Food Network. If you cook with a sense of rhythm it will impose restraints and balances.

I listen to the same kind of dance music when I am driving because it keeps me alert. The rest of the time it's usually jazz or classical.

TRP: As with rhythm, there are parallels between cooking and music. Say composition. How do you compose with colors, flavors, textures?

MK: What cooking has in common with music, painting, writing is that it is about finding a perfect balance. Too far one way or the other is always a mistake. The trick is in finding that perfect balance. I also think there are color rules to cooking. Two foods whose colors clash will have clashing flavors as well.

TRP: How do you plan a menu?

MK: My menus are sonatas that begin with an allegro movement. The third movement needs a surprise.

TRP: You're kind of a purist, for example, your amazing book *Cod*, which uses one fish as a lens for a good chunk of world history. If you had to eat only one food for rest of your life, what would it be?

MK: I want to say fruits because they are so beautiful and succulent,

TRP: Is there any kind of music that you hate?

MK: I hate the fake rock and roll that corporations such as Disney are feeding to kids. What is the use of rock and roll if it isn't raw and if it isn't angry? If it's corporate and easy like music for shopping malls?

MK: I have played piano, alto sax, and glockenspiel, but that is all well in the past. I was in school bands and orchestras—an experience sufficient to last a lifetime. Now, I play the cello almost every day that I am not traveling and I just do it for myself and it gives me enormous pleasure.

> " *I listen to music with a good dance beat because it imposes a rhythm, which is important when you are cooking . . . If you cook with a sense of rhythm it will impose restraints and balances.* "

such a complete sensuous pleasure. But not a very complete diet. I might have to go with vegetables which are also visual and offer tremendous variety.

TRP: What about one piece of music?

MK: Bach, though I would struggle choosing between the Well-Tempered Clavier and the cello suites.

TRP: Who would you be if you were a rock star?

MK: Mick Jagger, the Muhammad Ali of rock who has been doing it so well for so long that he can sail through on nothing but experience now.

TRP: Word on the street is that you play some cello. How's that going? Any other instruments?

TRP: What's the most important thing to remember about the food world—and all the hype that surrounds it?

MK: It takes the fun out of eating when too much importance is attached to cooking and cooks. It's all getting taken much too seriously and is producing a lot of really bad food. ⁂

My career as an avant-garde chamber-music composer began with a crush on a tuba player.

Make that eight tuba players. The Manchester Tuba Octet had come to a small venue in London to perform new works for eight tubas. The musicians sat in a semi-circle, holding their cumbersome brass instruments with grace and exceptional good looks. There was the barrel-chested one with the shaved head, the tall slender one with the Cary Grant hair, and the blond with biceps that suggested he played rugby as well as music. Between each piece, the eight of them cracked jokes about modern composers and tubas. Regardless, I wanted to take all of them home with me.

I was 21. I'd been studying composition for nine years. I'd come to London for the summer before finishing college to try composing as my job. The city had such a vibrant new music scene, I figured if I couldn't enjoy writing there, I wouldn't enjoy it anywhere.

The friend I'd come with knew a few of the tuba boys, so we joined them for lagers after the show. At the pub, two of the musicians put their mobiles on the table to impress me (this was 1997, back when mobiles could impress). When one asked for my mobile number, I panicked and stammered the truth, that I didn't have a mobile. In my alarm I forgot I could just give him my home phone number. But it was too late: I sounded too standoffish for him to ask me out.

The next morning, I came up with a new plan. So I had blown my chance for a date; I could get another chance by writing a piece for eight tubas. Musicians like girls who write music. All I needed was a night job that would let me compose during the day.

I'd recently eaten at Chez Panisse for the first time, and as much as I loved the food, I couldn't stop watching the kitchen: None of the cooks said a word as they worked. I was shy and often found talking a struggle. If it was possible to have a job where you could fill eight hours creatively in total silence, I wanted that job. With uncharacteristic boldness, I called a few London restaurants to ask if they could use an extra pair of hands. The British chef at a nearby French hotel restaurant said to stop in the next afternoon.

The front desk clerk escorted me to the kitchen. The small room was filled with steam, clanging pots and a blur of men in white jackets and blue aprons. From the mists the head chef emerged: A tall, slender man with a kind face, he looked a bit like the Cary Grant tuba player, but for the Uncle-Fester-esque shadows under his eyes. He was only 28 but had been cooking since he was 14. He walked me out to the dining room for a brief interview.

Emily Kaiser Thelin
VIRGIN IN THE KITCHEN

His name was Martin Hadden, but I'd come to know him as Chef. He kept the interview short. "I need a room service cook to make simple things. Burgers and tuna sandwiches, mostly. You look like you could handle a tuna sandwich, yes?"

I nodded.

"I'm more concerned about my boys. They've never worked with a girl before." He nodded towards the kitchen. "I'll do what I can, but . . . ." He shrugged.

I'd glimpsed a few of the guys in the kitchen; they looked harmless enough. I changed and tied on an apron. Chef handed me off to Jason, his pastry chef. With a flop of streaked hair, he looked like a surfer with a strong south-England accent. He set out a block of dough next to a stack of the smallest tart shells I'd ever seen.

"These are for my petits-four, yeah?" he said, pulling off a wad of the pastry. "Press the dough down nice and thin. But don't leave your thumb in there too long, or else you'll melt the butter and make my tarts tough and cost us a Michelin star."

I looked to see if he was joking, but he wasn't. In fact the whole crew moved about in a grim panic. "We're in the shits," Jason whispered. "Service starts in less than an hour. Those boys are totally fucked."

"Someone turn on the radio," a dark-haired man shouted, whom I'd later learn was the sous-chef, Steve.

"We need all the help we can get."

Jason hit the switch. I can't recall what the track was; it might have been Donna Lewis' "I Love You Always Forever," or the Backstreet Boys' "As Long as You Love Me." It hardly mattered. The radio was tuned to a pop station. In my composition studies, I'd confined myself to atonal music written after 1945—the post-Schoenberg twelve-tone constructions of Milton Babbitt, for example, or the early tape pieces of Steve Reich. I hadn't listened to pop music since the age of 14. The synthesized beats and tightly crafted melodies piped through those tinny boom box speakers and rushed like heroin straight to my heart.

And I wasn't the only one. The collective mood lifted, and everyone quieted down. Even the waiters found excuses to share the sudden good mood, as a few of them came into the kitchen to help polish the wine glasses. A kind of order emerged from the rush as the chefs set up their stations for service. I didn't look around the kitchen so much as pan across it like a film camera. I felt as though I'd walked into the full-color cinematography of a movie—one with a fantastic soundtrack and a happy ending.

"Who is this playing?" I asked Jason as the next song started. It reminded me of Motown, but even cooler.

"It's Jamiroquai, silly," he said. "Wait, you don't know Jamiroquai? What music do they play in America?" I laughed. "I don't listen to the radio much."

"What do you like then?"

"Um, mostly 15th-century choral music," I said. "And some more modern stuff—"

"Fifteenth century choral music!" he said slowly but sharply, like a game show host announcing a new category. "Who the bloody hell are you?"

"Emily?"

"Well, you've got good thumbs, we know that much." Jason said, as he pulled the baked shells out of the oven.

And promptly shattered it. Shards of pastry and lumps of cream splattered onto the counter below.

But when I looked up, no one had spotted my mistake. I took a deep breath and started humming along softly. I wiped up the mess and swirled the cream into another shell. In my music writing, I could struggle for weeks to generate pieces no longer than four or five minutes. But here in the kitchen, it took a half hour to fill the shells with cream. I topped each one with a trio of ripe blueberries, and nestled them into paper wrappers, then lined them up in a plastic tin to keep them fresh. I felt as though I'd written the first movement of a symphony. Service started just as the cooks finished prepping

" The synthesized beats and tightly crafted melodies rushed like heroin straight to my heart. "

Jason slipped the golden crusts out of their shells. Wafer-thin, they caught the light like stained-glass windows. I could hardly believe the beauty of our handiwork. Jason showed me how to swirl in pastry cream using a pastry bag and a fluted tip, then left me alone while he helped the crew suds down the kitchen before service.

I studied the pastry bag nervously. Another song came on, New Edition's "Something About You." The upbeat tune gave me courage. I picked up a shell and held it between the thumb and forefinger of my left hand while I carefully swirled the cream with my right. Growing more confident, I held the shell more firmly.

their stations. Chef instructed Jason to turn off the radio. A kind of spare, spoken music took its place as Chef called out the first orders. "Ça marche," he sang, French for "that walks." "Two scallops, two duck."

"Oui, chef," the entire kitchen answered, even the dishwashers. The three cooks on the line turned to their stoves. Sliding skillets onto their burners, they seared the scallops and duck breasts before submerging them in pots of clarified butter, keeping them moist as they finished cooking in the ovens (this was old-school French cuisine). Waiters came with silver cloches and white linen napkins to take the orders away.

The next day I dutifully rose to work on composition exercises, writing four-part harmonies in the style of Palestrina, a 16th-century Italian composer whose counterpoint methods were studied by Haydn, Mozart and Beethoven. I made plans to attend a BBC 3 performance at the radio station's studios. Then, I sat down to start my tuba piece. I played a few chords on the piano. I played a few more. I thought about the pieces the ensemble had played at the concert: fluid, inventive, confident. No matter how flawed my own writing might be, I tried to reassure myself, the octet would play the completed piece with flair. I wrote and rewrote and rewrote. I worked my eraser down to its metal casing. Until I realized: This is going nowhere. Why not head over to the restaurant a little early?

My shift started at 3. I showed up at 2:15. Looking pleased to see me, Chef told me to roast two chickens for the room service menu, as we'd run out of chicken salad for sandwiches. Per his instructions I greased the birds, seasoned them, tied their legs together and put them in the oven. Then I set to work forming tart shells for the petits-four, grooving to the gentle strains of Oasis and Radiohead. I forgot all about the chickens.

Two hours later Chef pulled the scorched carcasses from the oven. He banged the tray down on the counter—for all to see—then shot me a look of pure disgust. A part of me wanted to immediately evaporate from the earth, but another, smaller part of me held on. At the piano, with every wrong note I could sit and wonder if I should really bother to write music at all. In the kitchen there was no time for angst. Chef still

needed chicken for his room service sandwiches. I knew what I had to do. I just didn't want to draw any more attention to myself as I did it.

I went back into the walk-in and pulled two more chickens off the shelf. In the privacy of the pastry station, I greased, seasoned, and trussed again. I was about to sneak them into the ovens when "Vogue" started playing. That calculated, derivative tune is so goddamn catchy, I couldn't help but sing along. And bob my head. And maybe work my shoulders a little. "Strike a pose, there's nothing to it," I sang softly, encouraging myself along. As I snuck around the corner to slip the chickens into the oven, bam! I collided with Steve. I apologized but Steve started to laugh.

"Hey, look everybody! Emily thinks she's a regular Madonna!"

Everyone did look. Particularly once Steve started imitating the shoulder move. Chef laughed, too, and not in a very friendly way. "Don't burn those chickens!" he said.

Later that week, at a reception following the BBC 3 concert, I met a composer in her sixties or seventies. A plump woman with a big gray bun and a long gray cardigan, she looked like she'd wandered out of a children's book of Edwardian nannies. When she asked what I was doing in London, I explained I had come to try out life as a composer, and confided that I was having a hard time. Before I could explain the nature of my doubts, she interrupted.

"It's very hard," she said, swishing her wine glass a little too vigorously. "My god, I've been at it for what, 30 years? There's so little funding for the arts these days. The government doesn't care, no one cares. It's such a struggle to get paid to write anything, and then you get something performed and the only people who show up are other composers such as yourself. No offense, dearie, but I certainly understand your difficulties."

I thanked her for her time and lied that I needed to go meet a friend. I stepped out into the cool night air. In 30 years, was that the life I had to look forward to?

I started coming in to the restaurant earlier and earlier. I monitored the room service inventory and put in my own orders for chickens and cans of tuna. I bought a pair of chef's pants. I started learning some of the words to a few of the songs.

It didn't take long to memorize the full Virgin Radio canon. The station heavily rotated certain tracks, perhaps understanding that not all of its listeners were trapped in a kitchen for 15 hours a day. In fact two of our line cooks kept a running tally. Every morning they'd each pick a song: The Cardigans' "Lovefool," say, or The Verve's "Bitter Sweet Symphony." From 8:00 AM to 11:00 PM they'd keep count. Whoever's song played the most won.

The all-time record, funnily enough, went to an American tune —Jon Bon Jovi's "Midnight in Chelsea," a Bob Seger knockoff that got played 14 times in one day, or nearly once an hour. The only explanation had to be that listeners assumed Bon Jovi sang about their own London neighborhood. The British are patriotic about their Britpop in a way that Americans have never been about our own genres. Maybe Americans have too much Top 40 to choose from: country, hip-hop, hardcore, emo, the list goes on.

In our kitchen, as in the rest of Britain, each and every person embraced everything British on Virgin Radio. They knew long before I did that Boyzone came from the UK while the Backstreet Boys came from the US—and they liked Boyzone better. They liked The Verve, Radiohead, Lisa Stansfield and Jamiroquai because they were good, and because they were homegrown. They objected when Puff Daddy tinkered with "Every Breath You Take" for his tribute to The Notorious B.I.G., because an American had wreaked havoc with a British classic.

The cooks did have their limits, however. Oasis, then a rising rock band, had announced they were the new Beatles. A number of the cooks took umbrage with their hubris. Our Chef in particular thought they were brats. But Virgin Radio loved Oasis. Particularly the song "Don't Go Away," which was released late that summer.

In purely technical terms, in both its musical construction and its lyrics, "Don't Go Away" is a terrible song, one of several on *Be Here Now*, an album so disappointing that some credit it with bringing down Britpop altogether. The anthem carpets over embarrassingly predictable harmonic progressions with several shag rugs' worth of string orchestrations, while singer Liam Gallagher rolls around on the floor plaintively mewing terrible rhymes—or just repeating the same word over and over. "Don't go away, say what you say, but say that you'll stay, forever and a day, in the time of my life, cos I need more time, yes I need more time, just to make things right." It's awful, but when you put all those quibbles aside and just listen to it, the song still fills you with longing and hope. It makes you feel amazing and heartbroken all at once. As an emotional experience, it's brilliant. Noel Gallagher claims to have written it when his Mum thought she might have cancer. So it's also a little mushy. Maybe even a little girly. Which perhaps was always the problem with Britpop: It was

spat out a mouthful of tea leaves. Oh no, I thought, his bag must have torn. "You stupid cunt, do you read tea leaves, yea?" He dumped the leaves out.

Everyone in the kitchen stopped. Chef looked up from butchering salmon, Steve from scoring his duck breasts, Jason from thumbing his petits-four, even the two Nigerian dishwashers turned around from the sinks, holding their partially-washed pots.

My only explanation for what happened next is that Tina Turner's "Simply the Best" came on, infusing me with woman-power strength. From out of nowhere my inner Gordon Ramsay came flying out. "Yea, I do read tea

> **" Chef pulled the scorched carcasses from the oven, then shot me a look of pure disgust. "**

a bit fey. That might be why Dan the meat chef took such offense.

With his shaved head, Vandyke beard and scowling blue eyes, Dan scared the shit out of me—and I was taller than him, a lot taller. Unfortunately, it was the responsibility of the junior member of the kitchen (aka me) to make tea for the crew each shift. The British cooks had high expectations when it came to their afternoon cuppa, particularly Dan. On this particular afternoon, I served the Darjeeling with milk and a touch of sugar to Chef first; he took a sip and nodded his approval. I handed off the cup with milk no sugar to Steve. Then I gave Dan his black. He took a sip and

leaves, Dan, and yours say you're a fucking Scottish poof!"

At first Dan reared back as though he'd been slapped. Then he broke into a grin.

"You're alright, you are!" he said.

"Nice one, Emily!" Steve said. The whole kitchen cheered. Now, obviously I would never in a million years use the word "poof" in its classic sense. I despise homophobia in all its forms, and I'm not proud I had such success with it—even in the kitchen, where the chefs called each other poofs so often it qualified as a term of endearment. But from then on, Dan and I became great friends. In fact the whole kitchen changed. They didn't push me around nearly as much.

Over the next few weeks I fell into a routine. In the mornings before work I'd sit at the keyboard, finish my exercises and try to write my tuba piece. The dissonant chords, however meditative and thoughtful, sounded hollow and lonely compared to the melodies streaming out of that tiny boom box at work. That woman at the concert was right, I began to believe. Avant-garde compositions spoke to almost no one but friends of the composers writing them.

But more importantly, I felt so happy cooking. I could never share music with my friends in all the ways that I could share food. Music took weeks to finish, and days to rehearse and perform, for four or five fleeting moments of cerebral pleasure. Meanwhile, with petits-four alone I nourished and delighted dozens of restaurant customers. I brought home the end-pieces of foie gras terrines to my friends. I wowed my neighbors with my homemade bread, and showed off how to crack eggs single-handed.

And then came the dishwater dunking. On Chef's night off, according to tradition, the cooks held a lottery to pick a lucky waiter to torment. One night they asked me to pick the name from a bread basket filled with torn pieces of paper.

I stuck in my hand and drew the winner, a tall Frenchman named Patric. Steve instructed the other waiters to push back the racks of plates by the dish-washer and clear a space. As soon as Patric stepped into the kitchen (and he stalled for over an hour) the cooks jumped him. Five of them went at him at once, wrestling him to the ground until they managed to pick him up by his legs and arms and dump him into the pot sink filled with the night's washing water. Naturally, we had to console him with a few—okay 12—cold lagers.

The next night, Chef found me in the walk-in checking over my inventory. "Everything go okay last night?" he said.

"Yes Chef," I said uneasily, wondering if I might be in trouble for drawing the name.

"I heard the boys got a little rowdy."

"They were fine."

"Well, I think it's time you learned how to make a salad," he grinned, pointing to the bucket of freshly washed mixed greens. I was speechless. Even if it was as the cold side salad chef, Chef was promoting me onto the line.

He showed me how to dress the leaves, brushing them against the side of the bowl with my fingertips to avoid bruising. Then he demonstrated how to gently drop the leaves onto the plate, to give the salad shape and height—engineering miniature Eiffel towers of leaves. The following week, on the Chef's night's off, Steve ran the line and the cooks started to fall into the weeds. When an order came in for five appetizers off the hot line and two salads, Steve looked so tense, I hated to interrupt him to ask if I should make them, so I went ahead and made them on my own.

When it came time for the waiters to bring the order to the dining room, Steve knew the hot appetizers were ready, but didn't see the greens. "Two salads," he said, "I need two salads, who's got the fucking salads, you poofs!"

"Here, Chef, they're here," I said, pointing to the bowls piled high with red romaine, frisee and radicchio.

Steve stared. "Whey, Emily!" he bellowed. "Carry on like that and you'll get kissed!"

Thankfully Steve didn't make good on his threat. But that night, at home, I put down my pencil. I've never written another note since.

For the rest of that summer, I remained the appetizer chef, responsible for the cold starters and room service orders. As for the Oasis question, I decided to remain neutral. Except for Saturday football matches, the radio stayed locked on Virgin. Then one afternoon, for only the third or fourth time since the morning, the station cued up "Don't Go Away."

"Ah, great song!" the fish chef Luke shouted from the fish station. Luke adored Oasis.

In the middle of the kitchen, closer to the radio, Dan had been maneuvering a massive stock pot across the floor to start reducing his demi-glace. As the band lurched into the chorus, Dan scowled. He reached up for the radio as though the boom box were a large rat, with the tuning knob its head, and Dan was going to twist it off.

"You bloody bastard, don't you dare change the station," Luke shouted as he dropped his knife, hurtled himself over the counter and seized Dan around his thick neck. Luke had no chance. The other cooks barely had time to shout out their bets ("Fiver on Dan!") before Dan had Luke pinned.

"My glasses Dan, you wouldn't hit a man with glasses, would you?" Luke called out from the tiles, laughing. His ploy had worked. In the time it had taken for Dan to pin him, the song had finished. The radio remained on Virgin the rest of the day. ⁘

San Francisco-based **Emily Kaiser Thelin** *has written for* Food & Wine *and* The Wall Street Journal *and was nominated for a James Beard Award as a co-author of* The Harney & Sons Guide to Tea. *On her iPod she proudly plays Jamiroquai, Oasis, and Donna Lewis'* Greatest Hits.

John Besh

No city does food better than New Orleans. And nobody does New Orleans better than John Besh. His flagship venue, August, has topped *Gourmet* magazine's "Best of" lists twice, and his five other restaurants, Besh Steak, Luke, La Provence, American Sector, and Domenica, wow diners with takes on old traditions (think Creole Matzo Ball Soup). His heroism is legendary. During Katrina, he paddled a boat through the flooded city, armed with a gun and turbo bags of dried food for survivors. He skis, scuba dives, appears on TV with the likes of Wynton Marsalis, and, occasionally, sleeps.

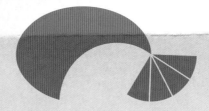

JOHN ★ BESH

Track 05
2:44 Mins

45 | RPM

SHRIMP
REMOULADE

J. Besh, M. Hearst & J. Camp
Produced by One Ring Zero

1 cup mayonnaise
1/4 cup Dijon mustard
2 tablespoons prepared horseradish
2 tablespoons chopped fresh parsley
1 shallot, minced
1 clove garlic, minced
1 tablespoon white wine vinegar
1 teaspoon fresh lemon juice

1 teaspoon hot sauce
1/2 teaspoon sweet paprika
1/4 teaspoon cayenne pepper
1/4 teaspoon garlic powder
Salt to taste

1 pound shrimp, peeled and deveined
6 cups baby arugula or mâche

For the remoulade sauce, combine the mayonnaise, mustard, horseradish, parsley, shallots, garlic, vinegar, lemon juice, hot sauce, paprika, cayenne, garlic powder, and salt in a large bowl and stir well.

Toss the shrimp in the remoulade sauce. Cover the bowl and let the shrimp marinate in the refrigerator for 1–2 hours. Serve the shrimp with the greens.

SERVES 12

It begins, like most good things, with drumsticks clacked together for a reverb-soaked four-count. But I'm getting ahead of myself.

When my daughter Iris was about eight months old, I took her out in the Baby Bjorn for one of our frequent walks down Broadway in Seattle. That's the same Broadway featured in hip-hop legend Sir Mix-a-Lot's classic, "Posse on Broadway," which I was probably muttering as we walked.

My posse was on its way to a little Russian meat pie bakery that is, sadly, now closed. (It didn't really sink in until I had to explain it to Iris that restaurants have a very short life span, and if you like one, enjoy it now, because soon it'll be too late, which seems like a reasonable philosophy for life in general.) When Iris and I got home, I put the baby and my beef-and-cabbage piroshky on the living room floor, warmed up Iris's bottle, and sat down for lunch. Iris didn't want the bottle. She wanted the piroshky. I knew this because she was staring at me exactly the way you would stare at me if I were eating a piroshky without offering you anything.

Matthew Amster-Burton
THE PIROSHKY EFFECT

After the piroshky was gone, I went around telling everybody about how my baby ate half a piroshky.

Me: "My baby ate a piroshky!"

Neighbor: "Congrats. I ate a sandwich."

In order to imbue this experience with some deeper meaning, I observed that there was something special about it: this was the first time Iris and I had enjoyed something in the same way. This was our first lunch date, the first time Iris and I had that human connection of experiencing the same auspicious sensory input (scientists call it the "piroshky-on-tongue stimulus") in the same way.

Over the next few months, Iris went on to eat her weight on a weekly basis in pad thai, enchiladas, sushi, and other hipster chow. But I realized recently that this wasn't really our first shared experience. To get there, we have to rewind several months to a period of my life I don't like to think about very much.

Lately it's become socially acceptable to complain about how hard it is to be a parent, which makes me feel slightly less guilty about what I'm about to say: having a newborn is just horrible. They are literally good for nothing. Iris was a relatively easy newborn, and it was still such a harrowing experience that my wife and I decided within a day or two that we were never having any other babies, and neither of us has ever felt like rescinding that hasty proclamation.

So one day in March, when Iris was between two and three months, I was home alone with the baby,

open. Then the voice of Joe Pernice: "Won't you come away with me / And begin something we can't understand." It took me a minute to realize that Iris had stopped crying. I paused the music. She wailed. I put it back on, and she stopped.

"The Weakest Shade of Blue" kicks off the Pernice Brothers' album *Yours, Mine & Ours.* It's the third record by the Boston-area pop group, and it came out in 2003, as did Iris. I still had it on heavy rotation by the following March, which is why it happened to be in the CD player. It's an urgent sort of tune. Obviously Beach Boys-influenced,

> **" Iris went on to eat her weight on a weekly basis in pad thai, enchiladas, and sushi "**

and the baby would not stop crying. I tried all the tricks. I let her suck on the tip of my little finger. I swung her around like a monkey. I performed several unnecessary diaper changes. I paced up and down the living room floor, bouncing Iris on my shoulder, crying along with her. I turned on the stereo not because I thought it would help, but because I was desperate to hear any sound other than screaming.

All of sudden: the drumsticks, the four-count. The guitar came in, slightly overdriven eighth-note power chords. The snare hit like an egg cracking

it never hits a loping bridge like a Brian Wilson song. It gets both verses out of the way before the chorus hits even once. It's probably coincidence that the pre-chorus goes "But don't cry, baby / Please don't cry, baby." I didn't reach for it for that reason, and Iris had no idea what it meant, but it worked on both of us. Iris and I looked at each other. I can't say for sure that she was thinking, "Wow, good song," but why else would she have stopped crying?

(Incidentally, I asked Joe Pernice's manager whether Pernice's kid has a favorite Pernice Brothers song and responds to it the same way mine did. "Joe doesn't spend a lot of time listening to his own music," she said. Oops.)

I can't say the song always worked after that point, but it became a tool in my arsenal, more potent than the monkey-swinging or finger-sucking. I never found another song that affected the young Iris in the same way, although I adopted another Pernice tune, "Working Girls," as Iris's time-for-nap song. At some point, approximately six million years later, Iris was no longer a newborn and had mostly stopped crying for no apparent reason, and her new love was books—board books that could survive chewing. She showed a little interest in John Vanderslice, the Shins, and Bloc Party, but only briefly, and started getting into Christmas carols and nursery rhymes. (Though if you're

Similarly, Iris's flirtation with grownup foods turned out to be a phase. As any experienced parent could have told me, babies will eat anything and two-year-olds will eat nothing. She lost interest in pad thai, spicy foods, and vegetables, and professed a fondness for cheese pizza and macaroni. Now we were from two different cultures. I'm always amazed at how young children, even those who don't spend much time with other kids, can absorb the cultural norms of their peers as if through the air. Nothing we could have done would have prevented Iris from getting involved with french fries and annoying songs, although I'm laughing imagining the reeducation campaign. Maybe sit the kid in front of a loop of Pearl Jam's "Jeremy" video. You will learn to be an individualist, or else!

" Nothing we could have done would have prevented Iris from getting involved with french fries and annoying songs "

sighing in relief that this isn't going to be one of those stories about how I taught my kid to love the Ramones and now she wears skinny jeans and is cooler than your stupid kid, maybe you should hop off here.)

For several years, Iris and I were like friends from different cultures. I could appreciate her interest in shitty nursery rhymes and nonspicy food, but I didn't really get it on a gut level. I don't want to overstate the case: we could always agree on Chinese potstickers and ice cream and certain amusement park rides and SpongeBob episodes. And I'm not saying that you have to get your kid to like the same stuff as you (like I said, not even possible) in order to really get along with them.

ed. When she fell for "The Tailor," I knew exactly how she felt. Iris also came back to sushi this year, and now we regularly stuff ourselves with eel and rice and seaweed, and moan with pleasure. Speaking as a guy, this is a rare experience, to

> **" This is my favorite thing about being alive, the ability to get swoony over a song, or a piece of sushi "**

But it sure is nice when it happens, isn't it? Which is why I was floored one day when Iris, age 6, was sitting on the living room couch, reading a book, and suddenly looked up and said, "Play that song again." I hadn't even been particularly listening, but I restarted the track. I could lie and say it was "The Weakest Shade of Blue," but it wasn't; it was "The Tailor," from Blitzen Trapper's 2010 album *Destroyer of the Void*. It starts with some lonely twanging guitar and the lyric, "I'm a long way from my home / I was born on the raging sea." It builds slowly to a ripping but still folky outro that sounds like the raging sea itself. Iris fell into a deep fairy-tale love-at-first-listen with the song. She restarted it a dozen times and taught herself the lyrics on the spot.

This is my favorite thing about being alive, the ability to get swoony over a song, or a piece of sushi, in a way that is so sudden and uncomplicat-

know for certain what someone is feeling, to be able to read her face like a headline.

Iris has her own playlist now and can drag her favorite songs onto it whenever she wants. In case Tipper Gore is reading, it includes Robyn's duet with Snoop Dogg, "U Should Know Better" (chorus: "You should know better than to fuck with me"), and another Blitzen Trapper song called "Black River Killer," a classic murder ballad about a guy who just can't stop killing people.

Iris reports that "Black River Killer" is currently her favorite song. She keeps a copy of the lyrics in her room. Neighbors describe her as a loner. ⠿

Matthew Amster-Burton *has written about food for* The Wall Street Journal, Gourmet, *and* The Seattle Times; *he's the author of* Hungry Monkey: A Food-Loving Father's Quest to Raise an Adventurous Eater.

Michael Harlan Turkell, once an aspiring chef, is now the culinary world's fave food photographer. He's shot such blockbuster tomes as *The New Brooklyn Cookbook* and the *Clinton St. Baking Company Cookbook.* He's the photo editor of *Edible Brooklyn* and *Edible Manhattan,* the genius behind the photo series "Back of the House," and hosts *The Food Seen* on HeritageRadioNetwork.com. Plus, he owns a cat named Mason who has a beer named after him–Sixpoint Craft Ales' *Mason's Black Wheat*. Here, Turkell's take on jazz and chicken.

Michael Harlan Turkell
TUNISIAN-TINGED
DRUMSTICKS

"The frenetic nature of Art Blakey's rendition of 'A Night in Tunisia' has made it a long-time favorite tune of mine. I love how Blakey broke away from Dizzy Gillespie's more fantastical and safe-seeming bebop, adding grit to the sound and strut to the song's pendulate time sequence. The pace reminds me of the feeling of cooking in a restaurant kitchen, in which I spent many years. If executing a recipe is a series of solos, that chorus together is an ensemble. Blakey sets up his mise-en-place one ingredient at a time. And slowly, methodically, all the forces harmoniously come together, creating a final dish.

"The sounds—the splatter of the oil, the clicking of the tongs—brought me to the idea of frying chicken drumsticks. This recipe is inspired by the spices of Tunisia, where harissa is as popular as ketchup is here— and it's so simple to make. It feels foreign, but aside from the little heat from the peppers, and spice from seeds, there's a familiarity to hot sauce in general. The dipping sauce is a riff on blue cheese, but again takes a nod from North African flavors, using yogurt to cool your palate, honey to sweeten, and orange blossom to bring out the floral notes of the spices. I find cooking to song soothing, but as an added bonus I've timed the steps with certain beats and movements of the music, so you can try this recipe at tempo."

3 ounces dried guajillo peppers
1/2 teaspoon caraway seeds
1/4 teaspoon cumin seeds
1/4 teaspoon coriander seeds
6 cloves garlic
Juice of one medium lemon
1/4 cup olive oil

1 cup plain Greek yogurt, strained
1 tablespoon honey
1 tablespoon orange blossom water
8 skin-on chicken drumsticks,
approximately 1 1/2 lbs
Salt to taste
1 stick (8 tablespoons) butter

HARISSA

Place the dried peppers in a bowl, pour boiling water over to cover. Let stand 30 minutes until softened. Deseed and destem the peppers. Pat dry with paper towel. Toast the caraway, cumin, and coriander seeds in dry frying pan over medium heat for 1-2 minutes, or until fragrant.

Place the peppers in a food processor. Add the garlic, lemon juice, and seeds. Puree until mixture is smooth. With machine running, slowly add the olive oil in a steady stream. Add salt to taste.

HONEY-ORANGE BLOSSOM YOGURT

In a small bowl, stir together the yogurt, honey, and orange blossom water.

DIRECTIONS

Pat the chicken drumsticks with paper towel until dry and sprinkle liberally with salt. Melt the butter in a large frying pan over low heat. When the butter is completely melted, using a spoon, skim the white milk solids from the top. Stir the butter and allow any remaining milk solids to rise to the surface. Skim those off as well.

Cue up the 12-minute version of Art Blakey and The Jazz Messengers' "A Night in Tunisia." Raise the frying pan to medium-high heat. Carefully place the drumsticks into the hot butter. At the 2-minute mark, when the drums break and the horns solo, turn drumsticks using tongs. Notice how the sputtering butter sounds like drums. At the 4-minute mark, when the piano transitions to the bass solo and the drums keep rhythm, turn the heat down to medium. Gently shake the pan back and forth occasionally, turning the drumsticks to coat.

When the high horns come in at around 10 1/2 minutes, reduce heat to medium-low. Put 3 tablespoons of the harissa in one side of the frying pan. Mix with the butter until incorporated using tongs. At 11 minutes, coat drumsticks with harissa butter mixture. Allow the sauce to reduce with drumsticks in the pan, turning to coat. Check chicken for doneness; if it needs more time, finish in a 350 degree oven for several minutes. Serve with honey-orange blossom yogurt.

David Chang

is the head chef and co-owner of multiple Manhattan
mainstays, namely Momofuku Noodle Bar, Momofuku Ko,
Momofuku Ssäm Bar, and Má Pêche. Famous for his pork
buns and soft serve ice cream, Chang has a few house rules.
One, if you want fortune cookies or karaoke, try down the
street. Any street. Two, he takes no reservations, except for
parties of six who order a whole pork belly or two triple-
fried Korean chickens. And three, Pavement is the world's
greatest band. He is the author of the *Momofuku*
cookbook and has appeared in *Time* magazine's
100 Most Influential People of 2010.

DAVID★CHANG

Track 06
4:15 Mins

45 RPM

MAINE JONAH
CRAB CLAWS
***
with Yuzu Mayonnaise
D. Chang, J. Camp & M. Hearst
Guest Vocals: C. Gonson
Produced by One Ring Zero

4 pounds frozen Jonah crab claws
1 cup Kewpie mayonnaise
1/4 teaspoon green yuzu kosho (yuzu chile paste)
1 1/2 teaspoons bottled salted yuzu juice

**Defrost the crab claws
according to the shipper's directions.**

**Combine the mayonnaise, yuzu kosho, and yuzu juice
in a dipping bowl and mix well.**

Serve alongside the crab claws.

SERVES 4

DAVID CHANG
FRIED CHICKEN, DAVID BOWIE, AND GIRLFRIENDS WHO LIKE *DESPERATE HOUSEWIVES*

TRP: Let's say you weren't a famous chef—how many months of your life could you lose to music?

DC: I have almost 2 years worth of continuous music on my computer. A lot of it comes from the restaurant—managers from bands come in and they're like, "Oh you're playing the band I represent!" and slide me some CDs. So my collection is a massive weird mix of stuff.

TRP: And you make your own playlists, right? How'd you come up with the bizarre mix of Nina Simone and Smokey Robinson for Má Pêche, your newest place in midtown Manhattan?

DC: We started playing music for cooks, not the customers! At Noodle Bar, we used to blast it just to keep awake. Really loud music is great to cook to, but it's weird because customers notice it, and pay more attention to the music than the food.

TRP: What type of music do you find most compatible with eating?

DC: Non-pop. You can play Yo La Tengo and 99 percent of the people have no idea who's singing, but it sounds good, so they're able to ignore it and focus on the food. As for us—the chefs—we usually go all night, so we need an eight or nine-hour-long playlist. I'm not gonna say we've exhausted the music industry, but there's very little out there that we haven't listened to.

TRP: You've got a kind of rock 'n roll crowd—when bands come into the restaurant, do you make a point to play their music?

DC: No! No no no, I make sure we don't play their music while they're there, it's embarrassing. And my other rule—we don't bother people. As wait staff, we have aspiring musicians and actors, and I will kill them if they approach anybody.

TRP: Which brings us to your temper. What's the worst temper tantrum you've ever thrown?

DC: I should be in jail. They're all bad. I literally black out in rage. It's like temporary insanity. It's bad for my health, so I haven't gotten mad—that mad—in a long time. Especially now that I'm rarely working service. Service is what kills me. On my feet, on the line. And after six years I just can't do the stress and perfectionism. I just want to make stuff.

TRP: Let's get pissed off now. What the fuck is wrong with food in America?

DC: With food, I love the very things I hate. Take the whole San Francisco thing. Rustic cuisine is great—it's one of my favorite foods. But when everyone's doing it, it's boring. Also, comfort food. I think it's great if some restaurants do it, but again, if every restaurant's serving meatloaf and mashed potatoes and biscuits, it's boring. I call that staff meal-ization. My chefs will go out to a restaurant and think, "This is our fuckin' staff meal! This is what we cook ourselves, between shifts!" I hate that sort of dumbing down of the culinary world.

TRP: Do you think the same thing is happening with music—it's getting dumbed down?

TRP: What about you—how do you compose your dishes? Some are so original, like cereal milk—toasted cornflakes steeped in milk, then strained—the milk is left with just a hint of salty sweet. How'd you come up with that?

DC: Right now, we have a lab where I spend most of my time. We want simple. Clear. We want a dish where people are like, "Fuck! Why didn't I

DC: It's a mixture of craft and art. It can be an art depending on how pretentious you want it to be. That's not the problem. It's the entertainment side of the business that you want to watch out for. There's a real distinction between an entertainer and a chef. I've said some terrible things about Guy Fieri (from *Minute to Win It,* on NBC). I said I'd throw him down the stairs and kill him. I said I'd throw him down again to

" It's the entertainment side of the business that you want to watch out for. "

DC: I'm sort of disenchanted with the current music scene. For example, someone just told me, "I love Kings of Leon." I was, like (dumbfounded expression). I'm not a musician, but I feel like the musicianship in music has disappeared. The artistry. I hate Top 40. Then again, music is complicated. It's so easy to slam Britney Spears and stuff. Sometimes it takes me years to appreciate something. I wasn't a huge Eminem fan until I actually listened to his stuff, and I was, like, wow—he's extraordinarily talented.

do that? It's so easy!" As a team, we've reached a point of saturation, not so different with music, where it's like . . . what do you do when everything's been done?

So we're focusing on things like rice. How can we get a better understanding of, say, a rice noodle, by making it from scratch without a stabilizer and high-tech machinery? By putting a creative limit or ceiling on what we can do, it forces us to really push the envelope.

TRP: Would you say cooking requires artistry? Is it even an art?

make sure. My oldest brother was like, "How can you make fun of Guy Fieri? He wears a wristband in honor of his son." And I was like, "If it really mattered that much to him, he wouldn't fucking tell anybody! It'd be just between him and his son." (Laughs)

This whole thing is a marketing ploy. Is it great for food? No, I don't think so. Then again, people do what they have to do. Take Rachael Ray. Rachael Ray busts her ass. She never proclaimed she was a chef, not once. She said that she just sort of stumbled into it. People wanna hate on her because she's massive—I used to be one of them. But Rachael Ray is fucking nice. She's driven. But nice. And I think our natural inclination is just to hate on people that are extraordinarily successful.

TRP: So many chefs are getting their shows on the Food Network. Are you saying the rock-star chef motif is incompatible with good cooking?

DC: Basically, it's the fame question, it's something I struggle with, because, I've been fortunate to have a lot of opportunities to do TV. I've done it when necessary. If you're on TV, it's your restaurant and your seats and you need asses in every seat. At the end of the day your restaurant's a business, at least in America.

Then again, I have a certain criteria about TV. And I feel like, if that criteria were met and I had the control to do it, then I'll probably do it. The first thing would be, is the show educational? Is it in the pursuit of knowledge? And the second, does it represent the restaurant in a good light? Not only a good light but an honest one. And the last one, does

it benefit research and development of new food ideas?

The emergence of the rock-star chef is a recent thing. If you're a good musician, if you're an athlete, if you're 5' 11" and 110 pounds and beautiful, you're gonna be a model, you sort of know in the history of culture what's going to happen. It's already been laid out a little bit. Before 2004, before the emergence of *Top Chef,* nobody knew anything. The most you hoped for was maybe your own restaurant. And then all of a sudden—you're going to be rich and famous? It changed the entire equation. It's gotten weird.

Cooking is no longer about cooking now. It's about trying to be famous. Or, even if you don't want to be famous, you know that that possibility exists. For cooks starting out, it's in their minds. Luckily, I started cooking before that really hit.

TRP: If you went out to see a band and had a few beers—okay 10 beers, what do you want to eat on the stumble home?

DC: My guilty drunken pleasure is chicken fingers. There's something

about the fried chicken finger. We're serving fried chicken at Noodle Bar—whole, no fingers. It was born out of a contest between Peter Serpico (the chef at Ko) and myself, about who could create the crispiest chicken. We both were just talking mad shit to each other. I was like, "This chicken is gonna break your fuckin' teeth . . ."

I made a Korean fried chicken—crazy popular all over Asia and America right now. It's a triple-fried bird, it's so crispy and spicy. Peter grew up in the Baltimore area, so he coated his in Old Bay seasoning. Anyway, we started this contest. A chicken-off. It took a couple months. And I think it ended a tie. I never wanna fry another bird in my life.

TRP: Have you ever considered cooking way, way, way outside your comfort zone? Like with something containing no fat?

DC: Fat-free, no. But seven or eight years ago, we would never be cooking *sous vide* or using hydro-colloids—which basically is a fancy word for shit that thickens food. Back then, I was like, "That's not cooking!"

Not only that but, if someone told me to add xanthan gum to a sauce, I'd be like, "No way." Or if they told me to measure it in grams and said, "Here's a gem scale," I'd be like, "I've seen gem scales before, they're not for fucking food."

And now I'm like, "Oh, this is a superior way to cook certain things." I think it's a great way to cook fish. I think it's a great way to cook some rice and meat, a great way to cook vegetables, make tofu, it's endless.

Because I realized it's all about the science. *Sous vide* helps you to have a better understanding of the cooking process. That's how I realized how ignorant I was. I had no idea why a steak gets brown, or burned for that matter—I cheated my way through chemistry and biology, and, well, high school. I don't know anything. I didn't learn anything. I know there's molecules and atoms and shit like that but . . .

LN: But what about more traditional techniques? Didn't you go to the French Culinary Institute?

DC: Old school cooking! It's got this manly thing. Cooking today has become much more gentle, much more finesse-oriented. And that can be misconstrued as not cooking. There's a lot of backlash against modern cooking, attacking stuff that Ferran Adrià or even Wiley Dufresne does, for instance. You can easily say, "That's just garbage. They call it, whatever, molecular gastronomy. It's a made-up name! It's fucking bullshit!"

But like Harold McGee said, gastronomy encompasses everything. I told everyone in my kitchens to make a concerted effort to understand things, even if we don't like them.

To go on a tangent, I remember when Gregg Allman was like, "This whole rap thing sucks! Rappers aren't musicians. They don't know how to play music. It's awful." Lo and behold they are musicians! Just in a completely different form. And with food over the past decade, it's been a slow process of learning more about the stuff that—even if I'd previously said, "I don't like that type of cuisine, I don't like that method of cooking"—I have to immerse myself in it, so I understand it. So if I'm going to criticize it, I'm at least knowledgeable about it.

TRP: Do you cook for girls?

DC: I have cooked for a girlfriend. When she was sick. Chicken soup. That kind of thing.

TRP: Did you check out her CD collection before you did it?

DC: Yeah. Kind of. Like one woman turned to me and said, "I need to see Lady Gaga." And I was like, "Ohhhhhh no . . ." What's that fucking TV show? *Desperate Housewives?* I dated this girl and normally— if it hadn't been that she was extraordinarily good-looking— there would have been all these red flags. But in my head I just kept thinking, it's going to be okay, it's going to be okay. And then, it just all built up—the bad music, the bad TV. And books too, it's like, "What? You're reading what? John Grisham!? What the fuck??"

TRP: I read that you are trademarking some of your really famous recipes like cereal milk?

DC: We did that for our pastry chef, because I thought that the recipe was original enough. You know people steal ideas all the time. And people have done that to us. We've seen photos of it. If we were walking through the grocery store and we saw, like, cereal milk by fucking Nestlé, I would've shot myself in the face, I would've been like, fuck me! So that's the main reason we did it, so we wouldn't kill ourselves.

TRP: Copyright protection doesn't do enough anymore, does it? For musicians or chefs. If they changed one word of your recipe, if I made, like, Rice Krispie milk, could you pursue me?

DC: The way I see it, in most cases, it's going to be promotion. I didn't understand when the Metallica guy Lars was like, "You can't pirate our music!" I think the more people have access to music or a kind of food, the more they're gonna crave it and gonna want it and they're gonna actually buy the CD or go to the restaurant. That's perfect for us. That's great marketing.

TRP: Do you play any instruments?

DC: As a kid, I played violin and trumpet and clarinet all at the same time. Terrible. Elementary, junior high stuff. My mom would never let me play guitar. That's all I wanted to play. Now I just wish I played the piano. It's actually useful. There's always a piano at like a wedding or a bar that nobody can fuckin' play . . . I can't even read music anymore.

TRP: Is there a musician you've never met that you always wanted to meet?

DC: I haven't met them but I've cooked for them. David Bowie—can I tell ya how cool he is? So fucking cool. And his wife. I mean, he is a very good-looking man. This guy was built to be a superstar. And Iman is just the most gorgeous woman. They're just radiating superstar shit. Crazy thing, I was at Craft and I was cooking for them, and Lou Reed's sitting at another table, and they didn't talk to each other! It was weird. But I would say the one guy who gave hope to every guy in the world is Ric Ocasek.

I wanna hang out with Ric Ocasek, with or without the rest of the Cars.

TRP: Do you ever wanna do anything else besides be a chef? Like be in a band?

DC: I want to fly-fish. Fly fishing is playing chess with nature.

TRP: Why is there ice in your urinals?

DC: So when you piss it doesn't splash. Because it's stainless steel, without it, the pee goes all over.

TRP: It's also kinda fun to watch the ice melt.

DC: Exactly. That's the main reason. I think it's one of the weird pleasures of being a guy is to watch ice melt, or snow melt, when you piss on it.

TRP: Do they put it in every morning?

DC: Every day, before service.

TRP: Do you have time to cook for yourself?

DC: I never cook for myself.

Songs to Lose Customers by
Songs on heavy rotation at Momofuku.

	Song	Artist	Album
1	*Chinatown*	Luna	Penthouse
2	*Margarita*	The Traveling Wilburys	The Traveling Wilburys, Vol. 1
3	*Sweet Lady Genevieve*	The Kinks	Preservation: Act 1
4	*Anything Could Happen*	The Clean	Anthology
5	*The Wild Kindness*	Silver Jews	American Water
6	*Work Hard/Play Hard*	Palace Music	Viva Last Blues
7	*Piece of My Heart*	Erma Franklin	
8	*Within Your Reach*	The Replacements	Hootenanny
9	*Coma Girl*	Joe Strummer & The Mescaleros	Streetcore
10	*Gone Head*	Asamov	And Now . . .
11	*Life Like*	The Rosebuds	Life Like
12	*Childhood's End*	Pink Floyd	Obscured by Clouds
13	*The Swimming Song*	Vetiver	Thing of the Past
14	*T.N.K. (Tomorrow Never Knows)*	801	801 Live
15	*I'm So Green*	Can	Ege Bamyasi

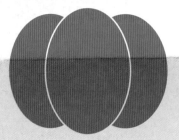

Andrea Reusing

Chef and co-owner of the Asian-inspired restaurant
Lantern in Chapel Hill, North Carolina, Andrea Reusing is
all about sustainable eating—and living. Her car runs on
leftover cooking oil. Her grocery list is simple: whatever's
in season. Her recipes grow from the local garden, with the
exception of anchovies, which she cannot do without. She
gets involved: Reusing serves on the boards of the Center
of Environmental Farming Systems and Chefs Collaborative.
She's won accolades from James Beard and *Grist's*
"15 Green Chefs" international list. Her first cookbook is
Cooking in the Moment: A Year of Seasonal Recipes.
She wants an ice-cream maker, bad.

45 RPM

Track 07
2:12 Mins

PICKLED PUMPKIN

A. Reusing, M. Hearst & J. Camp
Produced by One Ring Zero

Use small, firm organic pumpkins or winter squashes. Before peeling, slice
a piece and taste it with the skin. If it is tender, it can be left on.

3 pounds pumpkin, cut into thin moons or chunks.

Brine:
5 fresh Thai chiles, split in half lengthwise
1 small piece of unpeeled ginger, thinly sliced
6 cloves peeled garlic
10 white peppercorns
2 quarts unseasoned rice wine vinegar
1½ cups distilled white vinegar
1½ cups mirin
2½ cups white sugar
½ cup kosher salt

Combine the brine ingredients in a non-reactive pan and bring the mixture to a simmer.
When the sugar is dissolved, add pumpkin and cook gently,
checking frequently, until the pumpkin is just barely tender.

Cool in liquid and refrigerate.

SERVES 4

ANDREA REUSING
BRUCE SPRINGSTEEN, EGG HATERS, AND GIANT CLAMS

TRP: Tell us about your first love affair with music.

AR: I grew up in New Jersey. In Bergen County, in Glen Rock, which is about 15 miles from New York—a crucial 15 miles. So to be honest, I grew up as one of those horrible people that you run into on St. Patrick's Day who have cut school and are invading your classy Manhattan neighborhood. To visit the Irish pub.

So basically, I spent a lot of time at the Meadowlands, when Springsteen used to play there. We were five 16-year-old girls. I had this one friend who had really long nails and she'd always have a special manicure, and everyone had a perm, and we'd literally stand there at the gate. And stand there and stand there. Finally someone

would usually let us in.
Also my dad is a Dylan freak, so, a lot of Dylan in our house. Then there was the Who, and the Rolling Stones, so I was like a rock kid. To me that's the music of my late single digits, the music I listened to from the time I was a child until I was an early teenager—I'm a little stunted in that. And in some ways that music has an emotional quality to me that's not replaceable by contemporary music.

TRP: And then, out of nowhere, you married an indie-music god? Actually, Mac McCaughan, co-founder of Merge Records and guitarist from the band Superchunk. How did that mix with the classic rock?

AR: Yeah, I married well. At this point Mac makes mixes for me. But that doesn't mean I'm

listening to new stuff. I listen, but it might be Allen Toussaint. When I'm picking my own music I listen to a lot of like late '80s early '90s New Zealand.

Right now this second, I'm listening to The Love Language a lot, the Shout Out Louds. And obviously it's hard not to say Arcade Fire. I love M. Ward and Zooey (Deschanel), what they're doing.

TRP What do you listen to in the kitchen, do you listen to some of that stuff while you're cooking?

AR I'm not usually in charge of the music in the kitchen, so we'll listen to a lot of Mexican heavy metal. And, until very recently, there was somebody who grew up in Mexico whose favorite band was America, and it was literally a struggle sometimes to get him to not put his America on; he had like every America album. On cassette.

TRP: What do you play on the floor?

AR: In the dining room, we have a little bit of a country music controversy. Some people can't

TRP: So, it might be a weird question, but how does an Irish girl from New Jersey end up cooking Japanese, Korean, and Asian food in North Carolina?

AR: It was all about economics. There were no Asian restaurants in town when we opened.

specific. And what I do often is just take the plunge and buy it, and then you've got it and you've gotta cook with it.

This week I made a trip up to Virginia, just to visit a bunch of people that have these really interesting farm-raised seafood

> **" I grew up as one of those horrible people that you run into on St. Patrick's Day who have cut school and are invading your classy Manhattan neighborhood. To visit the Irish pub. "**

stand anything vaguely rootsy. But the music really runs the whole gamut. We have a separate space that's the bar, so we do a little bit more indie rock back there and rock and roll standards, and then in the dining room it tends to be more like jazz. It's so hugely important to a restaurant's environment.

TRP. And yet, you've rocked it. Where do your ideas come from for new dishes?

AR They come usually from necessity. Somebody will have a lot of something, like a farmer. Or suddenly we'll be able to get a whole bunch of a weird ingredient, like really nice surf clams, or monkfish liver, something

operations—clams and oysters— but they're doing them in the ocean so they're really salty, not like on the bay side where a lot of shellfish is normally done. We were joking about clams because I'd been ordering clams from them for a while and I usually get these very small clams because people like tiny, tiny clams.

And they were saying, we heard you really like seafood and that you have a good restaurant and we were really surprised that you ordered those tiny flavorless clams.

clam fritters on the same plate, like a little one-two clam punch.

TRP: A clam duet. So do you think of cooking as composi-

this pork belly thing, frying this pork belly in lard, doing it with five-spice, but it needed a complement, we were doing it in big chunks and it needed

" Actually . . . well . . . I don't trust people who don't like eggs. Something that's so versatile but also so much itself is so appealing. "

They kind of threw down the gauntlet with me. And so I said "No! I want the clams that you guys like best!" And so I got 800 enormous clams. For clam lovers they're no problem, but my challenge now is to take these clams and make them into something that are more generally broadly appealing. Because they have amazing flavor but I think they're gonna scare some people. So I'm gonna make a spicy clear clam broth and serve it with a pile of

tion—mixing a little salty chewy clam with a little sweet—?

AR: I hate to say this, but I see it mostly from the point of view of cooking. You want balance, and things are either alive or they're not alive, and they either have an original sense or they don't. And there is that snap judgment involved as well.

Take the pickled pumpkin from your song. Well we were doing

something to not be just pork belly on the plate. And it was fall and people here grow lots of big hearty squashes, that's what you get a lot of in the late fall. So we were doing the pork belly with five-spice and so it had star anise in it, and so that pickled pumpkin was a good complement to that dish.

TR: If you had to eat only one food for the rest of your life, what would it be?

AR: That sounds like a life-shortening question. But I really like eggs. Eggs can do so many different things, they can go so many different places. They're always this essentially very pure thing. Actually . . . well . . . I don't trust people who don't like eggs. Something that's so versatile but also so much itself is so appealing.

TRP: If you had to listen to only one album or piece of music for the rest of your life, what would it be?

TRP: What about new stuff? Any interesting flavors you're working on?

AR: We did a flavor last year that was kind of fun, it was apple cider vinegar to go with this hot heirloom apple dessert. That was really good. We do an ice cream—this is not original really—flavored with cherry pits. You crack them, you infuse them into the cream and so it has that bitter almond flavor. You have to be careful not to breathe the steam coming off

AR: No. (Laughs) I've only done karaoke once and it was . . . very late at night. I can't even remember what I sang. We used to have lots of karaoke parties at Lantern. In fact, three or four years ago, we had this one and Mac was doing a duet with one of my good friends and I went and grabbed the microphone. Mistake.

RP: And yet, did you have the rocker-girl hair, with the bangs in the front and all that?

> **" One of my favorite records is Big Star's Radio City. I have a weird tolerance for a lot of repetition, both with food and in music. I can play/cook stuff over and over and over. "**

AR: No idea. But one of my favorite records is Big Star's *Radio City.* I have a weird tolerance for a lot of repetition, both with food and in music. I can play/cook stuff over and over and over.

the cream because it has a little whiff of cyanide in it.

TRP: Let's get back to you and Springsteen. Did you ever dream of singing backup for the Boss?

AR: I'm not going to deny that there was a time I did own a crimping iron. ⠿

I grew up in the suburbs, in Stow, Ohio, which meant that some of the most vivid aspects of my education were conducted in cars.

I drove a beloved Nissan Sentra that entered my life in the wake of a bronze Toyota Corolla I'd dispatched two weeks after getting my driver's license. The Nissan was silver, or maybe gray—storm, let's call it. It was everything I'd ever wanted in a car: power windows and tape deck. Also, it had a stick shift, which I believed lent a certain procedural cool to the whole package.

Most teenagers get their first cars and seek any excuse to drive. Instead, I preferred my friends to chauffeur on weekends so that I could drink: cheap beer, tequila shots, and the boozy chunks of fruit from a bucket of "hairy buffalo," an unholy mix of fruit punch and random bottles of alcohol. I loved being transported, whether by crowds or cars or substances. The only exception was when, in the wake of some break-up or romantic encounter or other earth-shaking moment, I drove alone, smoking, with a dozen or more cassette tapes laid out on the empty passenger seat beside me.

Michelle Wildgen
THE ORDER OF DESIRE

Such a drive required preparation; I had to be sure each tape was rewound to the exact right spot, the only song I wanted to hear. (I found an organizational pleasure in cassettes that had my favorite songs—the ominous mournful songs, the ragey operatic songs, the songs obsessed with sex in some thrilling unsavory way—clustered at the end of one side and beginning of the next.) As I played each one I'd toss the finished tape over my shoulder and into the backseat, so that I could reach over and pick out the next cassette without taking my eyes off the road. I set up the tapes in a grid according to the order of desire, beginning with the songs I wanted to hear first at the top left. From there, I moved downwards, and eventually to the right. Out of the corner of my eye were visible the gradations in ivory and clear gray plastic, the typefaces and the logos, but I knew almost by touch whether it was *Nothing's Shocking* or *Ten,* Rush or Led Zeppelin; I knew the clear gray of *Blood on the Tracks* and the homely yellowed-tooth color of *The Very Best of Cream.*

When I actually prepared this whole set-up, I can't recall: Did I storm out of the house after a fight on the telephone and then sit in the driveway, setting up tapes for my cathartic drive? Did I get as far as a nearby parking lot and then meticulously, sobbingly, lay out the evening's soundtrack? I don't know. Frankly, both scenarios sound like something I would have done.

What I do remember is that the urge to hear certain songs was a need as physical as hunger, high volume as satisfying as consuming something salty and rich. I preferred music that left me jittery and amped instead of soothed. I felt "Layla"

This was the year I was learning to cook. I'd begun thanks to Nora Ephron's *Heartburn*, which described a dish I'd never tasted and could not quite imagine: hot pasta tossed with cool fresh tomatoes, torn basil, and olive oil, perfumed with a halved clove of garlic. I had never felt an urge to cook before, but curiosity hooked me into cooking this dish as easily as it had beckoned me in so many other directions. I dated and drank out of curiosity, so why not cook for the same reason?

> **❝ I had never felt an urge to cook before, but curiosity hooked me into cooking this dish as easily as it had beckoned me in so many other directions. I dated and drank out of curiosity, so why not cook for the same reason? ❞**

as a soaring beneath my diaphragm, some Jane's Addiction songs as a thrumming pulse in the throat and others as a wallop up my spine, Nirvana's "Come as You Are" as a sinister, sinuous pacing. Maybe everyone in my high school felt this way, though we never articulated it other than to say what bands we liked or hated. Certainly we needed it: music gave us our road map; it laid out the narrative and the rhythm for sex and attraction and break-ups.

(The pasta, it must be said, was addictive. I made it after school at least once a week for two years. I still make it, as does all of Italy.)

I learned a little about cooking from my mother, but mostly from magazines, where I was drawn to dishes that seemed, in their sophistication, to encapsulate an entire distant life. But I rarely shared my endeavors with anyone outside my family: as far as I can recall, teenagers in Stow, Ohio, hated eating in front of each other, at least in front of the opposite gender. We only did so when we were forced by prom and circumstance, or on nights we had nowhere to gather and so completed a circuit of the parking lots of the same shitty restaurants. Still, if you consumed your cheeseburgers in the car with the tape deck blaring, you could get through it. If you actually entered a restaurant you were fucked, because a meal across a table from a boyfriend inevitably uncovered some awkwardness: they gobbled hot pizza, wincing, or you dropped tomato sauce on your shirt. A deserted dining room revealed how tenuous the connection really was without the bracing scrum of a crowded party or concert, and the fact that we could only order soda reminded us that we were not adults to anyone but ourselves. But we knew we were supposed to master this ritual of eating together. So, sometimes a group of couples would make dinner, but only in a parentless house where we could turn up the stereo, smoke joints, and drink beer while we cooked. When my longest relationship broke up, my boyfriend and I tried to end it as we thought adults did—we made pasta in cream sauce and danced to "Wild Horses." It felt stilted because it was, but what can I say? We were teenagers, and this was how we thought it was done.

⁂

The cliché is to say my late-night driving playlists were my life's soundtrack, but the music was my life's substance too: it was the excuse to feel whatever was gripping at me, the theater that justified the grandness of all my desires. On those nights when I'd set up my musical program on the passenger seat, I was always alone. I drove and I listened but I never went anywhere; I circled, peered into other cars, and smoked picturesquely. I rarely picked up a friend to join me or drove by the house of whatever boy I was fixated on—this was a solitary mood and other people would ruin it. For one thing, they'd sit on my playlist. But also they'd see this ritual for the self-important melodrama it really was.

And I adored melodrama. I drew my images of love from music videos, a ruinous influence that left me thinking fights were languid and painless and that everything was cooler if it happened in slow motion or with a backbeat. I longed for the day when, with sunglasses and a chic bag, I would climb stairs on a tarmac to board a small plane and leave my lover on a Caribbean island to mourn my departure. I suspected but did not yet accept that these notions were horseshit: in real life, fights were blotchy scuffles, if you tried to move in languid slow-mo your brother would appear and ask you what the hell you were doing, and while I have indeed climbed stairs to board a small plane on a tarmac while wearing sunglasses, adults know that this sort of thing generally occurs in places like Oshkosh, Wisconsin.

But every now and again the right song came on when I was with the right person, and I was sure we both felt it: the song would feel sexy, percussive, suggestive, as enveloping as humidity. That was why we needed such volume all the time, to try and create that sensation. At such moments, a door would open onto the imaginary soap opera in which I lived, and for a few minutes the world felt as dramatic and profound as I believed it should. The videos were right! Life was just like them.

When I returned from those wanderings in my car, sober and nervy from nicotine, sated but still feeling just a tiny bit Gloria Swanson, I usually darted straight up the stairs to shower. I could not

and well-planned, and I was loath to extinguish it by chatting with my mom.

On the weekends, though, when I returned from dates or parties still pulsing with the beat of the last song, I was usually happily buzzed when I locked the front door behind me and strolled into the darkened house. My parents would be sleeping upstairs, the roaring attic fan muffling any sounds as I bumped into a table. I didn't want to end whatever giddiness I felt those nights by going straight to bed, but it was dark and quiet and I had to find something other than loud music on which to concentrate until

> **" Whole nights—whole years—seem to have passed this way, nothing but one big want: hunger, for some sensation or another, for everything. "**

encounter my parents, who failed to see the inherent drama in my love life and fixated instead on the trailing scent of tobacco. More importantly, I took great care to conclude my drives with the proper emotion—a playlist needed arc. It had to begin as wrathfully or tragically as possible and stay there for a good half-dozen songs before quieting, maybe moving from rage to a sly, patient simmer, or from keening to pale and tremulous acceptance. The point is, the final note of the evening's program still sounded in my head; that note was hard-won

I could sleep. Whole nights—whole years—seem to have passed this way, nothing but one big want: hunger, for some sensation or another, for everything.

If as a 10-year-old I'd only wanted a little Olivia Newton-John and a dish of softened ice cream, now I wanted texture and complexity, a little ugliness in my music and sharpness in my food, a little roughness and darkness. The contrast of that steaming pasta with cold garlicky tomatoes must have awakened some new appetite. I began to page through my food magazines more carefully, examining the dishes but also the people. Who were the cooks who served rich tangles of linguine with crabmeat and shiitakes, or bitter, pungent salads of artichoke hearts and radicchio? Maybe the same ones who loped out onto the tarmac to catch a plane; maybe people who weren't too nervous to converse with a boyfriend over dinner instead of hollering at a party; maybe novelists, sophisticates, and saxophone players; maybe, someday, me.

My late-night snacks became increasingly elaborate. I made hamburgers with Dijon mustard and romaine lettuce on a toasted onion bagel; I seared leftover salmon and placed it atop warmed sourdough with a shower of vinegary capers. It was not uncommon for 3 AM to find me humming under my

These rituals, both the driving and the cooking, were about appetite and desire, but what I remember most now is the pleasure of aloneness. I was learning that I loved to cook, but the skill did not strike me as a social plus. Except for that uncertain kiss-off meal I'd shared with one boyfriend, my cooking was generally a solitary thing. I'd come home from class and dice tomatoes, tear basil, setting them into a bowl to steep with garlic and olive oil while I boiled water. I liked being alone in the house, my shirt untucked, my parents at work, the dogs weaving around my legs looking for handouts and attention. I liked the sensation of procedure and competence in the same way I liked driving a stick shift or singing all the lyrics to a song. Not everyone knew how to do this, but I did. These were feints toward adulthood, incomplete and wispy, but they felt substantial to me.

" I circled, peered into other cars, and smoked picturesquely. "

breath and sautéing onions and sliced mushrooms. I must have cleaned up after myself, or else I would have heard about it, but no one ever asked, and so I had the feeling that no one had any idea what I did when I came home.

The older you get, the gentler the pull toward a song that articulates a sensation for you—it's less necessary when you've learned to do so for yourself. You lose that feeling of singular discovery, but I suppose you gain some dignity by no longer relying on Poison to define your emotions.

And yet just when I thought I'd achieved some new level of maturity, I'd be reminded how things stood. I was always distracted, and sometimes it mattered: the way I lost that Toyota Corolla was angel hair with shrimp and champagne. Other tidbits like this came later—say, turning on the heater in an overheating car—and sometimes they were actually helpful.

66 *These rituals, both the driving and the cooking, were about appetite and desire, but what I remember most now is the pleasure of aloneness.* 99

by flipping through the stations for a good song as I drove, until I glanced up to see the bumper of a black sedan looming huge and unavoidable. Once I started olive oil with chili pepper flakes over a medium flame in a covered skillet, wandered off thinking about something else, and ignited a fireball when I lifted the cover.

In the face of these crises I was childish and flustered. I was slow to remember to smother the grease fire and even then did so with a brand new beach towel. I hit the black sedan and totaled both cars, then sat owl-eyed and silent in the back of a police car.

When the officer took my statement, I vaguely recalled some admonition not to admit responsibility, even after an accident that was indisputably my fault. This bit of useful, grown-up information had filtered into my hazy consciousness somehow, past the Guns N' Roses videos and a recipe for

I had no idea where these flashes of competence came from, and I was equally disconcerted and pleased when they worked. Such successes reminded me that the world outside my head operated independently of my fantasies. Someday someone was going to taste the dishes I cooked up in the middle of the night, and perhaps they would not find them at all exquisite. Someday I'd finally realize that other drivers could see into my car and glimpse the theatrics within. Bit by bit, I could begin to see beyond the smoky windshield of my little Nissan and the steamed-up windows of my parents' kitchen late at night: there was a larger, real adult universe out there, and it was creeping in. ❖

Michelle Wildgen is the author of the delicious novels You're Not You *and* But Not for Long. *Her work has also appeared in* O, the Oprah Magazine, The New York Times, *and* Best Food Writing 2004 *and* 2009.

Michael Symon

is a James Beard Award-winning chef, restaurateur, Food Network regular, and certified culinary bad-ass. He rocked the Cleveland restaurant scene with hot spots Lola and Lolita, and has since debuted three more award-winning eateries: Bar Symon, Roast Detroit, and The B Spot. His 2007 *Iron Chef* victory catapulted him to culinary stardom. But if anyone was born to be a star, it's this motorcycle-riding, pork-loving, Van Halen-worshipping family man with a killer imagination. Like burgers? Take ground beef, add pastrami, swiss cheese, coleslaw, and a brioche bun. The combination won Symon the Top Burger in America award. Sweet! And savory.

MICHAEL ★ SYMON

Track 8
3:53 Mins

45 | RPM

OCTOPUS SALAD WITH
★★★
BLACK-EYED PEAS

M. Symon, J. Camp & M. Hearst
Produced by One Ring Zero

For the octopus:
2 tablespoons canola oil
1 whole octopus
1 gallon water
Juice of 2 lemons
Juice of 1 orange
1 cup white wine
¼ cup kosher salt
1 stick cinnamon
2 bay leaves
3 cloves garlic, peeled
1 onion, peeled and sliced
2 wine corks

For the marinade:
Octopus, from above
1 cup olive oil
2 cloves garlic, peeled and crushed
¼ cup red wine vinegar
Juice and zest of 1 lemon
1 sprig oregano

For the black-eyed peas:
20 Kalamata olives, pitted and halved
10 cherry tomatoes, halved
2 scallions, thinly sliced
1 cup cooked black-eyed peas
Salt and freshly ground black pepper to taste

For the garnish:
Parsley leaves
Thinly sliced red jalapeno peppers
Sea salt

For the octopus: In a large pot, heat oil over medium heat. Add octopus and cook until octopus releases its liquid. Add remaining ingredients, bring to boil and simmer until octopus is tender, about one hour. Remove from liquid and let cool.

For the marinade: Place octopus in a non-reactive container. In bowl, whisk together oil, garlic, vinegar and lemon juice and zest. Add oregano and pour over octopus. Cover and refrigerate overnight. Coarsely chop octopus and reserve.

For the black-eyed peas: Combine olives, tomatoes, scallions, and black-eyed peas and season with salt and pepper.

To serve: Top black-eyed peas with octopus and drizzle with marinade. Garnish with parsley, peppers, and sea salt and serve.

SERVES 4

MICHAEL SYMON
RASPBERRIES, MOUSSAKA, AND METALLICA

TRP: You've been described as America's MVP of pork. You created a pork tailgating playbook. Is there a musical equivalent to your love of all things pork?

MS: Stevie Ray Vaughan. He's not my favorite musician but he's the musician that I could listen to constantly.

TRP: You've also been called a rock star chef. Would you say being a chef has helped you out—in the past—with the ladies?

MS: Well, I mean it scored me my wife 20 years ago. So it's worked out very well for me, yes. Thank you.

TRP: Do you two have a special romantic song?

MS: (Cackles) Johnny Cash. "Ring of Fire."

TRP: Tell me you used to want to be the other kind of rock star. Like with a band.

MS: When I was a kid I wanted to be like Jimmy Page or Eddie Van Halen. I tried to play a few instruments . . . incredibly unsuccessfully. Like, you know, the guitar. (Cackles) Couldn't play it.

TRP: And your favorite musician?

MS: Um, it would be . . . it would either be Led Zeppelin or Van Halen. My first big show, though, was Tom Petty and the Heartbreakers. I was 12 or 13. It was awesome.

TRP: How about the first major meal you ever attempted?

MS: You know I grew up around food so, I cooked with my Mom constantly as a kid. But probably the first like big fancy meal I cooked was the year

before culinary school, when I did Easter at my mom and dad's house.

It was a lot of pressure. If you're part Greek, Easter's a lot of pressure. (Laughs) I did leg of lamb. I did a moussaka, just a lot of the stuff my mom used to do. Everybody ended up happy. And you know I've been doing it ever since, so I guess that's a good sign.

TRP: Cleveland has been a pretty massive influence on you and on your cooking. Would you say it's done the same for your taste in music?

MS: It's the rock and roll capital of the world, damn it! (Cackles). I mean yeah, Cleveland is definitely a rock and roll city and my musical taste is definitely skewed that way. I love all music. I love rock and roll predominantly, but I listen to a lot of country, a lot of

Willie Nelson, I got a lot of Hank Williams on there, and Charlie Daniels. I listen to rap too.

I pretty much love everything except techno. That's a style of music that I just wish never came to be. And I was very excited when it left.

TRP: So what about the Rock and Roll Hall of Fame? A lot of people have issues with putting

of Americana, it's a great thing. My father loved music, which, you know, is one of the reasons I love music. And for me, as a kid growing up, learning about Pink Floyd and the Dead and the Beatles and bands like that from my Dad, it very much influenced my musical taste. And you know my stepson, when he was growing up and loved punk, me turning him on to Stevie Ray Vaughan and Zeppelin and

the 1972 Tour of whatever. And it's just cool to really see history through that. It makes you feel like you were there almost.

TRP: What's your position on music in your restaurants? What will I hear, say, at Lola, versus Roast?

MS: Both are pretty, you could say, upscale restaurants. But we're not afraid to play the

" Cleveland is definitely a rock and roll city and my musical taste is definitely skewed that way. "

rock music in a museum. What's your take?

MS: I love it. I go there quite a bit. I bring my little nephews there, cause they can learn about history. And I think whenever you get to see a glimpse of something that is so . . . kind

Van Halen very much influenced his musical taste. And I think when you can bring someone to museums, you can really kinda show him the generations of rock and roll.

My favorite area is where you can see what the Clash wore in

music that we love to listen to. You go to Lola, which is considered a fine dining restaurant, and Zeppelin will be on the rotation.

When we first opened 15 years ago, we were one of the few restaurants that played rock. So you'd get a lot of people complaining that it was so loud. My response was always, you know, everybody bitches about a loud restaurant but nobody ever comes back to a quiet one.

TRP: Some celebrity chefs out there are known for their tempers and you just always seem so chill. Even on *Iron Chef.* What's your secret?

MS: I just think that the people around me are more productive when I'm calm and I think I'm at my best when I'm calm. So you know, I think, typically the more volatile a chef is my guess is the more insecure they are too.

TRP: Is there something that really pushes you over the edge? What just pisses you off?

MS: (Laughs) Uhhh . . . god, I do not like repeating myself. I tell people when we hire 'em, "I'm going to tell you how to do it once, I might get to tell you how to do it twice, but if I have to tell

you how to do it three times, you probably shouldn't be workin' here." So I just kind of get it out there in a very honest fashion before we start. And then, you know, it keeps me from blowing up and it keeps our kitchen a very happy place.

TRP: You also have that awesome "No Whining" rule posted at B Side Burgers. Does that generally work?

MS: You know, the funny thing is the people that aren't whiners look at it and get it and they'll laugh because they think it's very funny. But then you still get the whining from the people that we hung the sign for. (Laughs) "What do you mean I can't whine, oh man!!" Some people are just happier when they bitch, and that's the bottom line.

TRP: Is there a food that you absolutely hate, one that might even drive you to whine?

MS: Raspberries.

TRP: Raspberries?

MS: Can't stand 'em. Hate 'em. Hated them since I was a child and still hate them today. It's pretty much the only thing I won't eat.

TRP: The only thing?

MS: I'm not a huge fan of kidneys. So I'd say raspberries and kidneys.

TRP: On the other hand, food and music can both be guilty pleasures. What are yours?

MS: When I was younger, there's like some bands that you kinda keep in your closet cause you don't want your friends to know you jam to 'em. So I would say that my guilty pleasure would probably be Journey and Bon Jovi. Both of them I loved—but not so openly until I got a little bit more comfortable with

> **"Chefs look at me a little cross-eyed when I say it but I am a fan of Miracle Whip. I grew up eating it 'cause my dad always put it on our sandwiches."**

myself. I grew up in a city called North Olmsted which was like the heavy metal capital of the world, so, you know, let me tell you something: Journey was all I could handle. ABBA, you know, was not on the radar.

My guilty pleasure food-wise? Chefs look at me a little cross-eyed when I say it but I am a fan of Miracle Whip. I grew up eating it cause my dad always put it on our sandwiches. And I would also have to say salt and vinegar chips with french onion dip.

TRP: What else was on the soundtrack to your childhood?

MS: My wife makes fun of me because my musical taste really hasn't changed in 40 years. I still love the same bands. Actually, it takes a lot for me to add a new band to the cycle. I love '60s, '70s, '80s rock.

The only newer band that I've really added, like heavily, to the cycle is Band of Horses.

TRP: You've got two seconds. Pick—classic rock or heavy metal?

MS: Uh, god! You know one plays off the other so it's hard for me. I love metal. (Laughs) I looove metal. I mean, god, if someone put a gun to my head I'd pick classic rock. But I love metal.

TRP: What's the world's most awesome metal band?

MS: Metallica. (Laughs)

TRP: I'm pretty confident that you've heard this before but you have a pretty remarkable laugh.

MS: The maniacal laughter (Laughs), yeah.

TRP: If Metallica was putting out a new album and wanted to feature your laugh on one of their tracks, would you be game?

MS: Yeah, for sure! A little evil cackle. ⁂

I grew up a fundamentalist Christian in a small town in New Hampshire.

Our religion wasn't the wild kind—no shrieking in tongues, no miracle healings, no poison serpents twisting around believers' hands and forearms. It was a New England type of hardcore Protestantism, the stuff of Hawthorne; distrustful of the whims and urges of the body; eyes on the end-of-times, which was about to happen, oh, any minute now. God was angry, vengeful, a God hazed in brimstone. The Bible was the literal truth.

Jonathan Dixon
A CULINARY HERETIC

As a teenager, I walked a weird and tight line, enamored to the end-strands of my DNA with the loucheness of the Rolling Stones, with the surreal daze of the Grateful Dead, Neil Young's wailing sorrow, but also wanting to get through the coming apocalypse and wind up unscathed. My parents didn't make it easy. They were true believers, devoted, but they were also kind of different from the other members. My father is an artist. My mother works with non-profit organizations. On Saturdays, my father would often pick out some of his favorite records and give them to me. On Sundays we were in church. So while I waited for the end to arrive, I also set about amassing a monstrously large music collection and spent hour after hour in its sway.

I remember being at a weekend retreat for church youth, at about the age of 14, in the cold of a Massachusetts autumn. Somehow, during recreation time, the topic of music came up. A few kids confessed that they liked hearing Crosby, Stills, and Nash or the Eagles when they came on the radio. I mentioned the vast stacks of vinyl in my room.

"My dad gave me all of his," I said. "Hendrix, Dylan, Zeppelin, the Stones. I've been getting my hands on all the Grateful Dead I can. I'll make you guys tapes if you want."

One of the kids looked at me funny: "Wait—your dad gave you records?"

"Yes. A lot of records."

"The Rolling Stones . . . the Grateful Dead . . . Led Zeppelin . . . don't those people take drugs?"

"Yeah, indeed they do."

He eyed me with a bleary look of pity and contempt. "Once that stuff gets into your head," he warned, "it changes you. You need to keep your mind clean, keep your brain as pure as possible."

Did this make me some kind of heretic? The name "Satan" originates from a word meaning "adversary," which means someone who distracts your gaze from the path of righteousness. Which I guess, in my world, made Keith Richards Satan. And I kept listening to him.

⁘

and leaps into a motion faster than understanding. It carries on relentless—coiling and coiling—and doesn't stop and doesn't stop until it does stop, braking and breaking into nothing at the end. For me, it was a new way to feel, and my senses didn't know what to do. The experience of hearing it was the experience of a thousand volts surging through a 10-volt transistor, and I wished that all of my life was that moment replicated, end on end on end.

It did not have the force of revelation, but I knew at that moment, as certain as I was of the sun setting that night, that I was not a believer.

> ❝ Satan originates from a word meaning 'adversary,' which means someone who distracts your gaze from the path of righteousness. ❞

There came a definitive event. During the summer of 1986, I bought an album by Black Flag, *Damaged*, and in the dreary stifle of my room, I wound up playing the record over and over and over, as if it were some alien artifact fallen down from Venus or something.

One song in particular—"Depression"—obsessed me with its streamed heat and noise and blinding light. What lyrics there were didn't matter; all that counted was the scrape of the husk of the voice evacuating the throat. The song begins with a drone

⁘

I went to college in Boston, away from home and away from church for the first time in my life. And, perhaps predictably, went a little nuts pursuing women and cheap drinks. I loved my freedom. I also missed my parents, and felt not just a little bit adrift away from the strictures of the Word. I started cooking for myself as much as I could to recreate the tastes of home.

My parents were great cooks and passed their knowledge along. They taught me the basics: roasting a chicken and making rich gravies, how to make Yorkshire pudding that rose up like a mountain range. But I went at cooking now with

gave them a charge, my parents never quite understood the point of expending so much thought and effort on analyzing records or performances. But cooking they understood. There wasn't any question over the importance of food.

"I went at cooking with the same obsessiveness that bulked up my record collection"

the same obsessiveness that bulked up my record collection. It took over.

This is a commonplace pathology: a rabid enthusiasm expands to the point where a person's old form of living can't contain it anymore. In the realm of the spiritual, this is what causes people to become clergy. In my case, it caused me to, years later, spend hours cooking or poring over a cookbook collection that started, size-wise, to equal my record collection. Marcella Hazan, back issues of *Gourmet* magazine, *The New York Times Cookbook*—I read and cooked through as much as I could.

For a while after college, I wrote about music for newspapers. Even if seeing my name in print

Behind the recipes in my cookbooks lay an esoteric but attainable body of knowledge, a set of food illuminations that I couldn't stand not knowing. Kitchen success had always been hit or miss, really good homemade pasta one night; an oily, sopping mess of a tempura the next, and I wanted the know-how—all the secrets—to make every meal sublime. I didn't know what I wanted to do with the knowledge beyond knowing it.

Eventually, I moved to an area near Hyde Park, New York, and enrolled at the Culinary Institute of America. I spent two years being initiated into the mysteries of the cult of the chef: learning how to cook sauces, knead dough, and generally make heat do what I wanted it to. I didn't quite wind up unscathed: one serious burn, and six stitches after I went hand-to-hand with a mandoline and lost the tussle. But I came out with an understanding, if not (definitely) a mastery, of how to make food do what I wanted it to. Which is another way of saying, how to make my life better on a day-by-day, meal-by-meal basis. I'm still working out the fine print. But I went because I wanted my life to be filled with moments like I had a few days ago: I ate at our friends' home a dinner that is already ascending in my memory to the status of the mythic. At a point in the future when the fates are counting down my remaining breaths on a single hand, I'll

the pig, coaxing it through its life on a diet of acorns and peanuts and apples.

And how can I even describe it? Those vegetables, that meat—it was what life—all of it, the crux of it—tastes like, every bite shimmering with heat and sweetness and the whole essence of the earth. The fat of that pig was like a fabric woven from Eden's mists. I ate and kept eating, blooming into the height and depth and breadth of the moment. My senses didn't know what to do. I had to keep closing my eyes.

The next morning, recollecting the dinner, I thought back to my Black Flag afternoon.

> **" I went hand-to-hand with a mandoline and lost the tussle. But I came out with an understanding, if not (definitely) a mastery, of how to make food do what I wanted it to. "**

remember that meal. There was red wine, vinted in Washington, full of spice and vigor. I was also served roasted butternut squash and brussels sprouts sautéed until caramelized and sprinkled with cumin and aleppo pepper. They brought to the table a portion of pork braised in white wine with rosemary. My friends had grown the sprouts and squash; a farmer in the Hudson Valley grew

The record. The meal. Maybe the brain distinguishes between the two experiences, but the senses don't. And the body just knows it's alive. ⁘

Jonathan Dixon *is the author of* Beaten, Seared, and Sauced, *an account of his time at the Culinary Institute of America. A former music critic, he splits his time between Brooklyn and the Hudson Valley.*

Tom Colicchio

sits atop pretty much every food chart you can name.
Five James Beard Foundation Medals. *Bon Appetit* Chef
of the Year in 2002. King Tut of *Top Chef* for nine seasons
running. He co-founded Gramercy Tavern, twice voted Most
Popular Restaurant in NYC by Zagat. His current eateries,
Craft, Witchcraft, and Colicchio & Sons, are adored by the
Manhattan throngs. Moreover, he's something of a superhero.
He successfully performed the Heimlich on Joan Nathan, an
award-winning cookbook author who was choking on a hunk
of chicken. He nourished rescue workers at Ground Zero. He
boxes and shoots tequila on occasion. Strums guitar at sunrise.
Publishes cookbooks, four and counting.

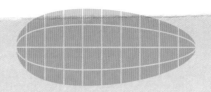

TOM★COLICCHIO

Track 09
3:10 Mins

45 RPM

CREAMLESS
CREAMED CORN

T. Colicchio, M. Hearst & J. Camp
Produced by One Ring Zero

12 ears of corn, shucked
Kosher salt and freshly ground black pepper
2 tablespoons unsalted butter (optional)

Using a hand grater, grate the kernels from 5 ears of corn into a bowl.
Press the grated corn through a fine sieve, reserving the "milk"
and discarding the grated corn and the cobs.

Cut the kernels from the remaining ears of corn. Combine the corn kernels, 1/4 cup water,
and salt and pepper in a medium pan. Cover the pan and steam over medium-low heat,
stirring once or twice, until the corn is tender, about 5 minutes.
Drain, then set the corn aside.

Stirring constantly, bring the corn "milk" to a simmer over medium heat in a medium
saucepan. Reduce the heat to medium-low and cook, continuing to stir, until the "milk"
thickens, about 3 minutes. Add the cooked corn, salt and pepper, and butter (if using)
and cook until the corn is heated through.

Serve warm.

SERVES 4

First of all, the cover. Pure white. Just like a clean white napkin, the kind you'd get in a fancy restaurant, where the waiter smoothes it out, almost inappropriately, across your adolescent lap.

You're 12 and you just bought your first Beatles album. *The White Album.* Your friends are fighting over Paul and John, John and Paul. A few Ringo and George enthusiasts even pop up at your junior high. You, however, can't stop thinking about "Piggies."

You think you see them at the table next to you in the fancy restaurant your parents take you to to celebrate somebody's birthday—not yours.

The swines are a matched pair. Mr. and Mrs., him in a bowtie, she in pearls, clutching forks and knives to eat the bacon—thick-cut and sizzling. You can smell the lard, golden brown, and your stomach growls.

This always happens when you think about the album. It makes you hungry. You see it as one big banquet, a savory feast. Surely that's how the Fab Four meant it: An extended foodie metaphor that becomes an earworm when you go out to dinner. You can't get it out of your head. You see it on every plate. And the Piggies seem to understand this. They tuck in, gleefully, with gusto, passionate about food, about life. You want to be at their table.

Melissa Clark

THE BEATLES' WHITE ALBUM: I'M JUST HERE FOR THE FOOD

But there you are with your family, dressed in your awkward pre-teen best, humming Beatles tunes and pretending you're not actually related to the people seated next to you. Not your aunt with the unfortunate dye job and steamed salmon fillet, sauce on the side. Not your sister, glumly reading *Betty and Veronica* comics under the table.

Your grandmother, far into her 70s, orders coffee with her appetizer. She sugars it, creams it, and sips it with her onion soup, topped with cheese as unctuous and oozing as the French waiter. She is the kind of person who eats just to live. You imagine her eating a Glass Onion. You hope she doesn't break her teeth. She paid a lot for them.

"She could have bought me a car with the money she spent on her teeth," your cousin once joked. Sort of. You like your cousin. She's a vegetarian, the only one you've ever met, which means she's eating pasta instead of the splayed Cornish hen on your plate. You admire the golden little bird which, with wings akimbo, looks like it got zapped mid-flight.

Stare at it long enough and you can see it right itself and take off again. Somehow it's got all its feathers back on, a sleek Blackbird singing in the dead of night, only waiting for its moment to be free. Like you. Waiting for dessert so that the meal could be over.

At least the Beatles are with you, keeping you company. You know you need to sit through dessert because it's someone's birthday (not yours). You scan the dessert menu, singing "Honey Pie", a fluffy Vaudeville-inspired number written by the cloying Paul.

But there is no pie. There is, however, ice cream. Not your favorite flavor, a conflation of "Rocky Raccoon" with "Why Don't We Do It in the Road." Rocky Road ice cream, marshmallow-riddled, sweet and drippy, melting on my fingers with little bits of raccoon fur embedded here and there . . .

That's when you realize the song doesn't actually mention cake. But in your mind the two are inseparable. How can there be a birthday without a cake? How can you possibly be related to these cake-denying people?

All of this bothers you all the way home. You still worship the Beatles . . . but. It's a nagging in the back of your mind. Where's the cake? Maybe you should jump ship and start a Rolling Stones obsession. What with all that Brown Sugar (at 12 you haven't paid attention to the lyrics). The *Let It Bleed* album cover. . . .

" *How can you be related to these cake-denying people?* "

Nor is there a Savoy Truffle. Or a creme tangerine, or Montelimar (which your adult self will Google and know, finally, means nougat). No ginger sling with a pineapple heart (whatever that is, it sounds like sugary bliss). George, the Beatle you would go for if you weren't so obsessed with the food, wrote "Savoy Truffle" in honor of Eric Clapton, who had the kind of sweet tooth you can relate to. The kind that waits, impatiently, for the end of this dinner, in part to get to dessert. You want dessert because it's sweet. But even sweeter is the post-dessert blackbird flight of freedom, soaring far away—as far as your little wings can take you—from your family.

Eventually, a birthday cake arrives at the table, encircled with burning candles. You say it's your Birthday. You sing and hum and strum and air guitar under the table as the cake is cut. Buttercream splats on your plate. Your grandmother puts her bony hand up, rejecting a piece.

Years go by, you still sometimes think of that moment, singing the Beatles' *White Album* at someone's birthday dinner. And it's still there now, miniscule, wedged in the folds of your brain. A birthday without cake. Your grandmother and her bright and shining fake teeth. As white as the album. She couldn't care less about cake. She was just happy to see a lifetime of coffee stains gone in one dental visit.

Three decades later, your teeth are stained with tea and red wine and every single birthday you've celebrated has had cake. And sometimes, in secret, maybe when you've had too much wine, you still think you see Piggies at the table next you; they're still enjoying the feast. ⠿

Melissa Clark *is the author of many cookbooks, including* In the Kitchen with A Good Appetite, *based on her* New York Times *dining section column.*

Aarón Sanchez

is the mastermind behind NYC's favorite Latino eateries,
Centrico and Paladar. He's also a television golden boy,
appearing on *Chopped, Melting Pot, Boy Meets Grill,
Iron Chef,* and, with Chris Cosentino, *Chefs vs. City*. His
primary culinary influence? His mother Zarela, founder of
the acclaimed Café Marimba. According to family legend,
cooking was supposed to be a disciplinary tactic for her
chico rebelde, but after tasting her son's deadly delicious
Pork Chops with Plums, Zarela knew he'd caught her bug. If
one female influence is good, two is better—the name of his
wife Ife Mora, lead singer of the afro-punk band SwEEtie,
is permanently doodled on his body. Twice.

AARÓN ★ SANCHEZ

45 RPM

Track 10
4:14 Mins

DUCK BREAST WITH
DULCE DE LECHE ANCHO CHILE GLAZE

A. Sanchez, J. Camp & M. Hearst
Produced by One Ring Zero

3 dried ancho chiles (1 1/4 ounces),
stemmed and seeded
2 cups boiling water
1 clove garlic, minced
1/2 cup freshly squeezed orange juice
1/4 cup prepared dulce de leche
1/2 cup homemade or store-bought
low-sodium chicken stock

6 Muscovy duck breast halves (3/4 pound
each), rinsed, patted dry, trimmed
of excess fat, and scored
Coarse salt and freshly ground black pepper
1 tablespoon unsalted butter
1 tablespoon chopped cilantro

Place chiles in a small, dry, heavy-bottomed skillet over medium heat, and toast until slightly darkened, turning once, about 40 seconds. Transfer to a small heatproof bowl and pour over boiling water. Let stand until softened, about 20 minutes. Using a slotted spoon, transfer chiles to the jar of a blender. Add 1 cup soaking liquid and garlic; blend until smooth. Set aside.

Place orange juice in a small saucepan over medium heat. Cook until liquid is reduced by half; add dulce de leche and chicken stock. Bring mixture to a simmer and immediately remove from heat; set aside.

Working in batches, season duck with salt and pepper and place, skin side down, in a large heavy-bottomed skillet over medium heat. As fat begins to render out, drain into a heatproof bowl and discard or save for another use. Continue cooking until skin is well-browned, about 15 minutes. Turn, and continue cooking duck until meat is browned, about 3 minutes more. Transfer duck to a plate and repeat process with remaining duck breasts.

Return all duck breasts to skillet, cover, and cook until an instant-read thermometer inserted horizontally in the center of a breast registers 135 degrees for medium-rare, about 6 minutes. Transfer duck to a carving board and let stand, uncovered. Pour out and discard all but 2 tablespoons fat from skillet. Add reserved chile and orange juice mixtures to skillet, along with any duck juices that have accumulated on the cutting board. Place over medium-high heat and cook, stirring, scraping up any browned bits that have accumulated in the bottom of the skillet, until thickened, about 6 minutes. Whisk in butter until melted. Season with salt and chopped cilantro. Slice duck breasts and serve immediately with sauce.

SERVES 6

JJ Goode

A WINE LOVER'S GUIDE TO MEXICAN MUSIC

Banda

A rollicking blend of brass and percussion, robustly structured with tuba and clarinet and an undercurrent of snare and bass drum. Leisurely late lunches at a fonda in a cacophonous market. A fine partner for tlacoyos and sopes with corn fungus or for sipping white burgundy.

Mariachi

Unpalatable to dilettantes, with boisterous, staccato trumpets flirting with guitarrón, violins, and the occasional yell. Garibaldi Square at night or the 7 train on a weekday. Match it with Mexican clichés done well: huevos rancheros, carne asada tacos, and mole poblano.

Ranchera

Mistaken for a varietal of mariachi, it is marked by a leisurely pace, blooming to elegant crescendos, often melancholy and featuring the multiple "llorando"s. It has legs and tannins. A flower-covered balcony, a lover walking away in slow motion. Perfect for solitary consumption along with tequila and a plate of chicharrón to drown sorrow with guilt.

Norteño

Straightforward and easygoing, accordion flavors dominate the palate, with hints of bajo sexto and serenading with notes of sorrow. A slow trip along a dusty road with friends and an amiable donkey. Serve with watery beer and a plate of rice and refried beans.

Narcocorrido

Like polka produced in Central American terroir, these ballads are punctuated by accordion riffs and tales of drug smuggling and pistol firing. A jaunty stroll through dark alleys in Sinaloa. Its lively acidity goes well with rich pork adobos, thick pipianes, and eight-balls of blow.

JJ Goode has written about food for Gourmet, Saveur, Food & Wine, *and* The New York Times. *He's co-author of* Truly Mexican *with Roberto Santibañez and* Simple Food, Big Flavor *with Aarón Sanchez. He often suffers from indigestion, which is the direct result of his fear that hot food will get cold and cold food will get warm if he doesn't eat it with all haste.*

Acknowledgments

Much gratitude goes to Jason Bitner, Kelly Eudailey, Claudia Gonson, Yonatan Israel, Jud Laghi, Fiona Maazel, and Nelly Reifler, who gave tireless feedback and support throughout the process; Sue Chan, Andrew Chason, Tatiana Graf, Liz Gunnison, and Pam Lewy, who helped us reach the people we needed when we needed them; Chris Cosentino, John T. Edge, Emily Kaiser Thelin, the Southern Foodways Alliance, and Mary Warner, who were instrumental in getting the ball rolling; Sasha Livitnov for her mad interviewing skills; Arjen Noordeman and Christie Wright who went above and beyond with designing such a beautiful package; Joe Beshenkovsky for the brilliant video work; Kate Sekules who championed us all over town; Elizabeth Koch, Lori Shine, and Lisa Sweet at Black Balloon Publishing who never stopped believing in such a ridiculous idea. Thank you so much!

Love,
Michael Hearst, Leigh Newman, and One Ring Zero

Liner Notes

One Ring Zero is: Joshua Camp and Michael Hearst
Vocals, accordion, claviola, keyboards, theremin, glockenspiel, guitar, drums, drum programming, bass, piano, triangle, and other noise-making devices.

Timothy Quigley played drums, and **Ian Riggs** played bass and sang backup on "Pickled Pumpkin."

Guest vocals by **Tanya Donelly** on "Peanut Butter Brunettes," and **Claudia Gonson** on "Maine Jonah Crab Claws with Yuzu Mayonnaise."

The One Ring Zero live band is **Joshua Camp, Michael Hearst, Ben Holmes, Ian Riggs, and Timothy Quigley.**

All songs recorded by Michael Hearst and Joshua Camp at Urban Geek Studios in Brooklyn, NY, except for "Pickled Pumpkin" which was recorded in Timothy Quigley's apartment in Brooklyn, NY, and the vocals for "Peanut Butter Brunettes," which were recorded at Gonsonheath in Cambridge, MA.

All songs published by One Ring Zero Publishing, BMI. ℗ and © 2011 One Ring Zero.
www.oneringzero.com

Contents by page number

P. 6   **Preface**   Leigh Newman

P. 8   **Introduction**   John T. Edge

P. 10   **Spaghetti with Sweet 100 Tomatoes recipe**   courtesy Mario Batali

P. 14   **Love and Caribou**   Christine Muhlke

P. 20   **Peanut Butter Brunettes recipe**   courtesy Isa Chandra Moskowitz

P. 24   **The Power of Popcake**   Kara Zuaro

P. 28   **The Ugly Muffin recipe**   Tanya Donelly

P. 30   **Brains and Eggs recipe**   courtesy Chris Cosentino

P. 34   **Chris Cosentino: Jane's Addiction, Pig Tripe, and Functional Insanity**

P. 38   **Raw Peach recipe**   courtesy Mark Kurlansky

P. 42   **Mark Kurlansky: Bach, Fake Rock, and Color-Clashing Vegetables**

P. 44   **Virgin in the Kitchen**   Emily Kaiser Thelin

P. 52   **Shrimp Remoulade recipe**   courtesy John Besh

P. 56   **The Piroshky Effect**   Matthew Amster-Burton

P. 60   **Tunisian Tinged Drumsticks recipe**   Michael Harlan Turkell

P. 62 **Maine Jonah Crab Claws with Yuzu Mayonnaise recipe**   courtesy David Chang

P. 66 **David Chang: Fried Chicken, David Bowie, and Girlfriends Who Like *Desperate Housewives***

P. 71 **Songs to Lose Customers By**   David Chang

P. 72 **Pickled Pumpkin recipe**   courtesy Andrea Reusing

P. 76 **Andrea Reusing: Bruce Springsteen, Egg Haters, and Giant Clams**

P. 80 **The Order of Desire**   Michelle Wildgen

P. 86 **Octopus Salad with Black-Eyed Peas recipe**   courtesy Michael Symon

P. 90 **Michael Symon: Raspberries, Moussaka, and Metallica**

P. 94 **A Culinary Heretic**   Jonathan Dixon

P. 98 **Creamless Creamed Corn recipe**   courtesy Tom Colicchio

P. 102 **The Beatles' White Album: I'm Just Here for the Food**   Melissa Clark

P. 104 **Duck Breast with Dulce de Leche Ancho Chile Glaze recipe**   courtesy Aaron Sanchez

P. 108 **A Wine Lover's Guide to Mexican Music**   JJ Goode

P. 110 **Acknowledgments, Liner Notes**

P. 116 **CD Tracklist**

Tracklist

1	Mario Batali's	**Spaghetti with Sweet 100 Tomatoes**
2	Isa Chandra Moskowitz's	**Peanut Butter Brunettes**
3	Chris Cosentino's	**Brains and Eggs**
4	Mark Kurlansky's	**Raw Peach**
5	John Besh's	**Shrimp Remoulade**
6	David Chang's	**Maine Jonah Crab Claws with Yuzu Mayonnaise**
7	Andrea Reusing's	**Pickled Pumpkin**
8	Michael Symon's	**Octopus Salad with Black-Eyed Peas**
9	Tom Colicchio's	**Creamless Creamed Corn**
10	Aarón Sanchez's	**Duck Breast with Dulce de Leche Ancho Chile Glaze**